Your Entrepreneurial Journey

Fifteen Guiding Principles

Second Edition

Your Entrepreneurial Journey

Fifteen Guiding Principles

Second Edition

WRITTEN BY
Michael D. Ames,
In collaboration with
John Bradley Jackson

EDITED BY
Linda Ames
Travis Lindsay

Pathways to Success Press
Newport Beach, California

Published by
Pathways to Success Press
1 Rue Cannes
Newport Beach, California

The opinions and proposals expressed in this book are the authors' alone and should not be interpreted as representing the views of California State University Fullerton or California State University Fullerton's Center for Entrepreneurship.

ISBN 978-1-7339315-1-9

Your Entrepreneurial Journey is the culmination of forty-five years of learning. Leaders of emerging, fast growth ventures have been our teachers. Also, we are grateful to be part of a community of many entrepreneurial voices – students, clients, faculty, volunteers and community leaders. We learn much from each other as we strive to improve. We hope our words accurately reflect the CSUF Entrepreneurship Community's collective wisdom. It is our privilege to write this book for them. This book will help you to succeed on your entrepreneurial journey. You will gain insights on developing your leadership potential, serving your community, and becoming the best that you can become. Mike and J.J.

Table of Contents

Acknowledgements

We give special thanks to the following members of our CSUF Entrepreneurship Community (We list in bold, all-caps the names of Current and Emeriti Advisory Board members. We list in bold the 156 co-authors of <u>Creating New Ventures: How to Shape Concepts Into Achievement (2018)</u>:
Christopher Aaron, Farouk Abdelwahed, Cecil Adams, Sam Afshar, **Rose Agracewicz**, Charles Almond, **Carla Amador**, **MICHAEL AMES** Parshant Amin, Ofer Amrami, Jnana Anderson, **Kelly Anderson**, Chris Anicich, Tom Apke, Greg Arbues, **Chad Armstrong**, **Jim Armstrong**, **Richard Aronson**, **Vas Arora**, Stuart Atkins, Catherine Atwong, **Joel Backaler**, Alexandra Backstrom, Charlie Baecker, Adrienne Bailey, **Andrew Baker**, Megan Baptista, Aaron Barkenhagen, Jeff Barovich, John Barrier, **Ken Bassman**, Russ Beale, Greg Beck, **Joey Beim**, Bill Bemus, Sue Bendheim, Ray Benedicktus, John Berger, Shelly Berggren, Alison Bergquist, **Michelle Bergquist**, Radha Bhattacharya, Jannine Bielesch, Stan Bigney, **Lorenzo Bizzi**, **DAN BLACK**, Jeff Black, Stuart Blake, Steve Blanc, Vicki Boatman, **James Bobbett**, **Daniela Anavitarte Bolzmann**, Carl Bozzo, Robert Bradley, John Brake, Chuck Breffle, Lourders Bray, **Rand Brenner**, Michael Brinda, Gary Brookshire, John Broussard, Earl Brown, Kira Cohen Bruno, April Buchner, Boris Bugarski, Marty Burbank, **Victor Bullara**, **Joseph Burke**, David Burt, **Jose Calero**, Evelyn Camacho, Sean Cantelon, Michael Capsuto, Earl Carbone, Mary Carbone, Glen Carnes, **Bill Carpou**, , Jim Carr, **Kevin Carr**. Ola Carr, **Terri Carr**, Rob Carrillo, **ANDREW CARROLL**, Mike Carroll, Brian

Cavanaugh, **Jim Cenname**, Ray Cerulli, Susan Cervantes, Michele Cesca, Greg Chagaris, Young Chai, Jim Chamberlin, **Curtis Chan**, Peng Chan, Ron Chang, Steve Charton, **Rudy Chavarria**, Betty Chavis, Wei-Cheng Chen, **John Chi**, **Jerome Chiaro**, **Eleni Mantalozi Christianson**, Kathy Coffey, Bill Cole, **Mark Collins**, **Jerry Conrey**, **Jim Cooper**, Bonnie Copeland, Will Cosmo, Linsey Crow, Mimi Ko Cruz, Bob Cryer, **Curt Cuscino**, Creg Cygan, **Zack Dafaallah**, Dale Dagley, Lee Daigle, Kirk Daley, Rex Danford, **Valerie Danzig**, Marilyn Darby, Paul David, James Davis, Daniel Decker, David DeFilippo, Kashyap Deliwala, **Christopher DeCaro**, Don Del Mazzio, **Suzanne DeRossett**, Tom Dexel, **Soheil Divani**, Loren Doll, **Rob Dorf**, Kathy Drake, Stephen Duarte, Ryan Dudley, Ellen Dumond, Bill Dyer, **William Dyer**, David Dyer, Elso Ebro, Mel Edwards, **Mike Edwards**, David Eisenman, **Micha Eizen**, **Matt Erickson**, Paul Estrada, **Brian Evans**, **Brent Evans**, **Ayisha Fareed**, Sean Fares, Tom Faust, **Deborah Ferber**, Gail Fernandez, Manny Fernandez, Jim Ferris, Reuben Fine, Brian Finnegan, Nancy Fisher, Thomas Fisher, **Derreck Ford**, Steve Forell, **Howard Forman**, Joe Formichelli, Linsey Fornaca, Richard Franzi, Howard Fraser, **James Fratzke**, **Ryan Fratzke**, **KARL FREELS**, Bill Friedrichs, Don Gage, Seraph Galeno, Charlie Gallagher, **Matthew Gallizzi**, Michael Gancar, Lawrence Gasman, Robert Gates, Bill Gobbell, Ray Godeke, **Bob Godlasky**, Jim Goff, **Ben Gold**, Scott Goldfarb, **Duane Gomer**, Maritza Gonzalez, Ricardo Gonzalez, Larry Gorum, Gene Grant, Bob Graul, Carolina Grechuta, Joseph Greco, **Jeff Greenberg**, Steve Gross, Ken Grossgold, Darryl Grubb, **KENNETH GUCHEREAU**, **Monica Gutierrez Hernandez**, **Michael Haddad**, **Munir Haddad**, Ronald Hankins, Tom Hardesty, Neil Harle, Marcia

Harrison, Ed Hart, Jason Hartman, **Theresa Smith Harvey**, Howard Hawkins, Jack Hayden, Dorothy Heide, **France Dixon Helfer**, Stephen Helper, Marieke Hensel, Jim Hensman, Alfred Herzing, **Rose Hickman**, **WALLY HICKS**, Greg Hill, **Nanciann Horvarh**, Paul Hugstad, Dorota Huizinga, John Ishimaru, Bob Jackovich, Heidi Meyers Jackson, **John Jackson**, **David Jafari**, **Dalip Jaggi**, Jack James, **Ken James**, **ROBERT JECHART**, Janice Jeng, Stephen Jester, Jitu Jhaveri, Charles Chao Jiang, Lori Johnson, Sue Johnson, Tom Johnson, Valerie Johnson, **Bowen Jones**, Chris Jones, **Greg Jordan**, Betty Jura, Sharon Kaak, John Kadletz, Barry Kahn, Sinan Kanatsiz, Carl Kasalek, Don Kasle, Ross Kaufman, Hilary Kaye, Kyle Keller, Rick Keller, Jim Kelton, Steve Kerpan, Steve Kerpan, Hong Kim, Geoffrey King, **Dave Kinnear**, Gaylord Kirksey, Chuck Kish, **Charles Kissel**, **Guy Knuf**, Bob Koch, **Teresa Koch**, Chiranjeev Kohli, Chris Kondo, Garrett Kop, **Robert Kovacev Sr**, **Rob Kovacev**, Kris Krabill, **Robert Kreisberg**, Mark Krikorian, Kathi Kruse, **Ash Kumra**, **Stephen LaCount**, Freeman LaFleur, William Liard, **Andy Lamb**, John Landgard, Irene Lange, Carl La Plante, Ron LaRosa, David Lautner, Charles Laverty, **Jesse Lawler**, Nate Lee, David Leibsohn, Amanda Leon, Kitty LeSage, **Randy LeSage**, Robert Lescaille, Stan Lewczyk, Matty Li, Linda Libriya, **Barry Lieberman**, **Jay Lieberman**, Ligaya Lim, **Travis Lindsay**, Robert Lippman, Angela Liu, **KRISTEN LLORENTE**, Tom Loftin, **Jeff Longshaw**, Melissa Lopez, Priscilla Lopez, **Virginia Lorimor**, Ciao Luu, Dennis Lyftogt, Elizabeth Macgregor, Chuck Macgregor, **Victor Macias**, Alicia Maciel, Lynn Mack, Daniel MacLeith, Judy Magargee, Paul Magargee, **RAJ MANEK**, **ALAN MANNASON**, Gus Manoochehri, Mark Mantey, Todd Marcelle, Sid

Marcos, Brent Marcus, Peter Margarita, Polina Marian, Steve Marion, Michelle Markham, Rey Marques, Jan Marshall, Chip Martin, Cheri Martinson, David Martinson, **Craig Martyn**, Kash Master, **Jonny May**, Diane Mazzey, William McClennen, **David McConnell**, David McCormick, Sue Pearson McCowan, Gin McCoy, **Don McCrea**, Todd McKnight, Pamela McLaren, Craig McLaughlin, Shari McMahan, **John "Jack" McSunas**, Ross Meader, **Charlesetta Medina**, Steven Mednick, **Sue Mehta**, Brian Mellen, Cory Mellody, Gary Melton, **Lynn Melton**, Marcy Mendez, **Angeli Menta**, Nancy Merlino, **Scott Merritt**, **Peter Meyers**, **Steven Mihaylo**, John Milane, Doug Miles, Daniel Milkie, George Miller, Nancy Miller, Tom Miller, **Mark Mitchell**, Jack Mixner, Robert Miyake**, Shruti Miyashiro**, Elie Monroe, Jim Monroe, Brian Montes, Bonni Montevecchi, Hector Montoya, **Bruce Moore**, Chad Morgan**, William Morland**, **DAVID MORRIS**, Grace Moyles, **Ryan Mueller**, Craig Mullin, Diana Munguia, Mike Murray, Jack Napoli, Derrell Ness, Thomas Nghiem, Michael Nguyen, Tam Nguyen, **Eric Niu**, Robert Nolan, Jan Norman, Tom Northup, **Scott O'Brien**, **David Obstfeld**, David M. Ochi, Donna Olpin, Scott Olpin, Jan Oncel, Jennifer Rudd O'Neil, Paul Oronoz, Ron Osajima, **Mark Packbaz**, **Niaz Panhwar**, Andrew Pardo, Paula Parker, **Clifton Passow**, **Ash Patel**, Deep Patel, Manish Patel, **Michelle Patterson**, Tom Patty, Ryan Paules, Jeff Paulin, Charles Pavia, Chuck Perry, Loren Peterson, Andy Peykoff, Vi Pham, Justin Phan, Hazel Phillips, Bob Pierson, **John Pietro**, Linda Pinson, Linda Piper, Dave Primac, John Primac, Ed Provost, Anil Puri, **Bill Purpura**, Kathy Pyle, Morteza Rahmatian, Jerry Ramos, **John Rau**, **NATALIA RAZEGHI**, Jim Rebensdorf, Christopher Reese, **LAURIE RESNICK**, Jack ReVelle, **JJ Richa**, Kit

Richard, Tyler Richardson, Rose Hickman Rigole, Gil Riley, **Arceli Rivas**, Jim Roberts, Jill Rodriguez, Byron Romig, Anita Ron, Dave Rothenbuehler, **ALI ROUSHANZAMIR**, **Shari, Rudolph, Nancy Russell**, Remoun Said, Allan Safahi, Teresa Saldivar, **Ron Saetermoe**, **Stacy Sagowitz**, **Sadaf Salout**, Barbara Samara, Frank Sammann, Hector Sanchez, Jose Sanchez, John Sandberg, Pete Saputo, **MICHAEL SAWITZ**, Molly Schmid, Ronald Schott, Jack Schrader, Gary Schultz, David Meerman Scott, Karl Seppala, Richard Sewell, Jigar Shah, J. R. Shaw, Deb Shea, **Steve Shields**, Mark Shultz, **Charles Simon**, Nirbhai Singh, Raj Singh, Earl Skakel, Masha Skolburg, Rich Skolburg, Ruth Smisko, Dan Smith, Edward Smith, Tim Smith, Bill Smyth, Sean Snider, Maria de Lourdes Sobrino, Cynthia Soriano, Jack Sorokin, **Scott Sorrell**, **Bernie Spear**, Richard Spielberg, Carol Spencer, Nancy Spiegel, Lisa Spillone, Terry Splane, Doug Sproal, **RONALD STEIN**, Gary Stell Jr., Jo Step, Diane Stern, Fred Stern, Bruce Stewart, Jim Stewart, **Phillip Stinis**, Dan Struve, Diane Struve, Bruce Stuart, **Chuck Su**, Richard Sudek, Scott Sussman, Sandy Sutton, **Sylvan Swartz**, Zack Swire, David Tabone, Anais Tangie, William Taormina, Kim Tarantino, Wayne Tate, Sheridan Tatsuno, Lynn Taylor, **Atul Teckchandani**, Valerie Teeter, Ben Thomas, Johnny Thomas, Ellen Thompson, **Oli Thordarson**, Joann Thoresen, Courtney Thurman, **John Tillquist**, **Aaron Tofani**, Ken Townsend, Tim Treloar, Jeff Trower, Mike Trueblood, Jack K.N. Tsai, Larry Tucker, **Ray Valencia**, Mike Valentine, Debra Valle, **Francisco Valle**, **JEFFREY S. VAN HARTE**, Moody Vashawaty, **Gonzalo Vasquez**, Ali Vaziri, **Johnathon Veta**, Gary Viano, **ARTHUR P. VILLA**, Brent Vinson, **Fritz Von Coelln**, Buzz Walker, David Walker, Greg Wallace,

Nicole Washington, Ray Way, **Shawn Way, Bruce Welch**, Shirley Welds, **Per Welinder**, Carl Wellenstein, Bruce Wells, Don West, Denise Westcott, Gregg Whitaker, John Widdows, Robert Wietzke, Dale Wight, **Michael Wilkerson**, Ellen Williams, Craig Willison, Robert Wittstock, Doug Wolfgram, Jeff Wong, **Tony Wong**, Carl Woodard, Dean Wright, George Wright, **Benjamin Yip**, Monte Yoder, Emeline Yong, Sandee Young, **Woody Young**, Fares Younis.

Introduction

This book is about your entrepreneurial journey. You jump start your journey when you use guiding principles to align your work and purpose. Your guiding principles will also help you to move forward. You will find that guiding principles help you achieve success by teaming with others. Successful entrepreneurs channel the incredible power of shared purpose and shared values. Everyone's satisfaction soars when the team's work and purpose align, even as everyone works harder than they ever imagined they could.

We know this because we have helped many, many entrepreneurs succeed. Experience has taught us that success is an entrepreneurial journey. Often we dream of a path forward, without understanding what success is for us. Or we are unclear about what we must do to align our capabilities with our dreams. For example, we often equate success with being the star player on a winning team. In truth, unwavering, determined practice of the fifteen guiding principles gains success. Successful entrepreneurs are not necessarily star players. They develop their leadership potential, serve their community, and become the best they can be.

Principled entrepreneurs provide exceptional value, feel great about their accomplishments, earn the respect of others, and achieve self-respect. We invite you to read this book and do the same.

The genesis of this book

Based on their collective wisdom, an entrepreneurial strategic planning committee derived the guiding principles presented in this book. The Center for Entrepreneurship ("CFE") at California State University Fullerton convened the prestigious committee. Appropriately, the committee was a diverse group as to background, age and their pathways to success. Almost everyone in the room was an entrepreneur. They had "seen the elephant" and they were there to give back.

The committee did not begin its work with discussion of a mission statement, a business plan or a business model. The committee prized the CFE's forty-year, successful track record. It was not seeking a new direction, or to turn things around. It sought to identify the CSUF Entrepreneurship Community's shared purpose and shared values. The committee knew that this "power grid" of shared purpose and value has incredible power. The committee wanted to "plug into" it and channel additional power to further advance the CFE's good work.

The committee members selected its novel starting point because they knew that if the CFE didn't "plug in" it would not continue to excel. Why?

Note: The CFE serves as an outreach center and support organization for entrepreneurs. It serves a vibrant local economy of approximately seven million people. Created by the Mihaylo College of Business and Economics, the center guides CSUF Entrepreneurship – a collection of entrepreneurial initiatives within Mihaylo College and campus wide. The CFE's reputation derives from decades of effective service to its community. The CSUF Entrepreneurship Community is an impressive assembly of entrepreneurs drawn from thousands of emerging, fast-growth ventures in and around Orange County, California. The community is a chorus of many voices. Members learn from each other. Together, they advance free enterprise and achieve enormous economic impact. Many benefit from CFE outreach.

First, consider the power of Purpose. The committee's task was to draft an elegant strategy for the CFE's future - a blueprint for building institutional success. However, they started by writing down their shared purpose. Why? They knew that they had to build on a purposeful foundation. They had to stay laser-focused on the CFE's purpose -- providing valuable recipes for success to founders of emerging, fast-growth ventures.

Tim Clark extends this blueprint-for-building comparison. In his book, Business Model YOU -- written in collaboration with Alexander Osterwalder and Yves Pigneur. Clark explains, "In order to create a blueprint, the architect must understand the Purpose of the building to be constructed. ... Purpose is equally important when [drafting strategy]. The organization's Purpose guides the design of its business model." He goes on to say, "Purpose is a crucial ... element. It is also a design constraint: After all, no organization – or building – can be designed to be all things to all people." (Clark, p.138)[1]

Clark also observes that at a personal level, "aligning one's work and Purpose jump-starts careers – and makes satisfaction soar."(ibid.) Alignment is a side

[1,2,3,4,5] See Intro-1 to 5 at
http://bit.ly/YourEntrepreneurialJourney

benefit that was well known to members of the strategic planning committee.

The committee agreed that The CFE's shared Purpose is "to be a leading voice for entrepreneurial growth, learning and action." More accurately, the "voice" is a chorus of many voices singing together as one.

Consider the power of shared Values. To the committee, the CFE is not a business organization. It is an ecosystem, a community of interacting stakeholders who understand the free enterprise system, and their physical environment. Two ideas from Daniel Priestley's book Entrepreneurial Revolution catch the essence of the committee's thinking.[2]

First, the actions of stakeholders in the CFE's ecosystem take aspiring entrepreneurs on a journey. They move from barely knowing what success is to feeling great about their accomplishments, earning the respect of others, and achieving self-respect. (Priestley, p. 144).

Second, the CFE's main assets are its intellectual properties (IP) – recipes for success that are mindful mixes of shared purpose and shared values. Priestly says it well. IP is "The special stuff that makes you valuable. ... your method of doing something, your unique philosophy behind what you do, the recipes for success that you know. It's your brand or reputation, it's your way of creating a culture that attracts top people. ... So how do you create more of it? How do you know what IP you already have but take for granted? How do you dig up this gold? You write." (Priestley, p.120)

As discussion began, the strategic planning committee's moderator recorded a flurry of ideas on the whiteboard. The shared values came forth as a mix of words, truisms, and quotable phrases. For example:

. Honesty
. Free enterprise s not just about making money
. Great enterprises create exceptional value
. Accept personal responsibility for strengthening our democratic institutions, becoming better citizens, and building our future.
. Be open to change.
. Have the courage to innovate, and the wisdom to build rather than destroy.
. Justice
. Peace
. Self-reliance
. Hard work to serve worthwhile ends.
. Walk the Talk

. Respect
. Success is a choice

The list needed work. The committee knew that how to energize purpose and employ shared values are the essence of the CFE's IP. The committee wanted IP upgraded in three ways.

First, the list of values had to inform the entrepreneur's purposeful journey. Combined, they needed to be a compass guiding progress. One that kept founders on their pathways to success. Pointing the way from barely knowing what success is to feeling great about accomplishments, earning the respect of others, and achieving self-respect.

Second, the list needed clarification of how one uses each value to build success. The clarifications had to be laser-focused on giving founders valuable recipes for success, not just giving them snapshots of champions.

Finally, the list needed expansion. It must stress that one achieves success within an ecosystem. The CSUF Entrepreneurship Community is a community of interacting stakeholders. They depend on the health of the free enterprise system, and the physical environment.

CFE staff accepted the committee's challenge. They invested many hours to transform the committee's list into an authoritative briefing on the CFE's essential IP. To do this and meet the strategic planning committee's three upgrade requirements, they converted the list into Fifteen Guiding Principles. The fifteen principles are recipes for success that are mindful mixes of shared purpose and shared values. Each principle contains action words and includes a supporting clarification statement. Chapter 1 presents the approved list.

When the strategic planning committee completed its work in June 2012, the Director of the CFE launched the Principled Entrepreneurship Project. The project strives to add value in three ways: (1) convey the full meaning of the CFE's Fifteen Guiding Principles, (2) clarify why we believe principled entrepreneurship is a success catalyst, and (3) share knowledge about how successful entrepreneurs use the Guiding Principles.

The project began by researching, editing and posting a series of twenty blogs over a one-year period. The first five blogs in the series helped entrepreneurs understand the need for purpose and Guiding Principles. Blogs six through twenty discussed the CFE's Fifteen Guiding Principles. Each blog stimulated entrepreneurial growth, learning and action. Content contained photos, links to valuable readings and videos, questions and exercises, all to help entrepreneurial readers concoct personalized recipes for success.

Reader responses to the blog series were positive and led to further research. CFE staff made several upgrades to blog content. In 2014, the CFE published the first edition of Your Entrepreneurial Journey: Fifteen Guiding Principles.[3] The center offered the book as a Kindle E-Book. The E-Book format provided the tech-savvy entrepreneurial reader with an affordable, full color presentation and hyperlinks to readings and videos. The first edition is still available on Amazon.com. Since then the Principled Entrepreneurship Project has learned much from the CFE's launch of the CSUF "startup" incubator in two locations.[4] The project has also done extensive fieldwork. In 2018 it produced a collaborative book with members of the CSUF Entrepreneurship community. The book is entitled, Creating New Ventures: How to Shape Concepts into Achievement.[5] The book includes 156 entrepreneur profiles and letters. The letters speak to future founders. The book is available in both full color and black and white printings on Amazon.com.

Today, the CFE's IP has increased in value. It is better at providing recipes for success that are mindful mixes of shared purpose and shared values. We have improved the CFE's published content. It better conveys meaning, clarifies why principled entrepreneurship is valuable, and illustrates how successful entrepreneurs use guiding principles. Every day, the CFE strives to advance its content from informational, to inspirational, to transformational. We have learned much in the last five years that will benefit you. We "open-source" our new learning in the second edition of <u>Your Entrepreneurial Journey</u>.

Even as you read this book, know that we strive to improve its value to you. The Principled Entrepreneurship Project is advancing to the next level in five ways. (1) We continue to collect original stories from the life experiences of people who have "seen the elephant." Stories that speak from the heart. Stories that describe the value of guiding principles to their professional and personal lives. (2) We interview role models. (3) We seek photo essays to support each principle. Essays that combine original images with captions and audio clips that tell the story. (4) We collect and curate original, 3-5 minute video clips that bring each principle to life. (5) We recruit volunteers. As we act, all roles are open. We need writers, interviewers, people to interview, editors, producers, and directors. We need moderators, panelists and coaches.

We invite you to join our ecosystem. Check out the CFE's IP address. It is:

(https://business.fullerton.edu/Center/Entrepreneurship/

We are a chorus of many voices. We help each other strive for success. Add your voice. Share your experiences and strengths. Together, we can help many entrepreneurs succeed, advance free enterprise and achieve enormous economic impact.

Interested? Contact us at:
https://business.fullerton.edu/Center/Entrepreneurship/Contact

Michael D. Ames
Founder and Chairman of the Board
CSUF Center for Entrepreneurship

John Bradley Jackson
Director
CSUF Center for Entrepreneurship

March, 2019

How to use this book

Learning more: Your Entrepreneurial Journey comes with a cloud-based *Resource Folder including footnotes with direct hyperlinks to third-party resources and other materials. The IP address for the archive is **https:bit.ly/yourentrepreneurialjourney***

Taking advantage of the direct links in the resource folder provides you two advantages: (1) direct links assure that you are a few clicks away from appropriate credit to photographers, video producers and authors that interest you, (2) direct links take you to details about the work, and often introduce you to other related works that will benefit you.

We believe that the two advantages of direct links outweigh two disadvantages: (1) the occasional inconvenience of having to navigate through ads to view content, somewhat like what you must do to enjoy a Network TV show. (2) dropped links due to the ever-changing face of the internet. Know that the links we supply are to help you explore, and not for our profit. If you encounter a dropped link we will help you find a new connection. Contact us at https://business.fullerton.edu/Center/Entrepreneurship/Contact

Chapter 1: Why Guiding Principles?

Lighthouse Island from the Mainland **CC by 2.0**
garlandcannon

In this chapter, we first list the CFE's Fifteen Guiding Principles. Each principle contains action words and includes a supporting clarification statement. Next, we explain why we believe Guiding Principles are essential to entrepreneurial success.

The CFE's Fifteen Guiding Principles:

1. Create Value - Create real, long-term value by economic means. Understand, develop and apply entrepreneurial practices to achieve superior results for stakeholders and for the community. Eliminate excess, waste, and unevenness to achieve performance and cost effectiveness. Ensure excellence in environmental, safety and all other areas of compliance – stop, think and ask.

2. Embrace Change - Envision what could be, challenge the status quo, and drive Joseph A. Schumpeter's "creative destruction," rather than being run over by it.

3. Apply Creativity - Challenge conventional approaches by applying curiosity, experimentation and discovery to solve real world issues. Embrace and encourage learning through hands-on, service-based learning with dynamic, entrepreneurial companies and student startups.

4. Celebrate Uniqueness - Each of us has a special purpose in life and it is no accident that we are on this planet. Each of us has unique skills. It is your responsibility to discover your purpose and do your best to fulfill it by developing and employing your skills.

14

5. Build Community - No entrepreneur has ever succeeded on his/her own. Find out what people need. Study larger community concerns. Make people's lives better while consuming fewer resources, leaving more resources available to satisfy other community needs. Certainly, reward your people according to the value they create for the venture. However, do not forget to also reward them for resource conservation and renewal.

6. Maintain Personal Integrity and Trust - Keep the promises you make to others and to yourself. Be the person that others can rely upon and place confidence in, both in good times and bad.

7. Be Aware of Right and Wrong - Do good. Never lie, never cheat, never steal. Conduct all affairs lawfully and with integrity. Everyone deserves to be treated fairly.

8. Love Learning, Wisdom, and Truth - Have the courage to kindle your desire to learn. Find lessons and inspiration in the success of others. As Charles Koch writes, "seek and use the best knowledge and proactively share your knowledge while embracing a challenge process. Measure profitability where practical." Adopt the elements of Carol Dweck's growth mind-set. Your greatest power is free-will. You possess the power of choice. For any endeavor, choose to develop your intelligence through determined practice aided by selection of good coaches. Effort is the path to mastery. Embrace challenges and persist in the face of setbacks. Most all good things come through adversity.

9. Practice Humility and Intellectual honesty - Constantly seek to understand and constructively deal with reality to create real value and achieve personal improvement. Actively seek criticism and learn from it. Don't whine, don't complain, and don't make excuses.

10. Be Caring and Compassionate - Principled entrepreneurs succeed by helping others to succeed. You cannot live a perfect day without doing something for another without thought of something in return. Give to others unconditionally.

11. Value Justice and Peace - Justice is the fair administration of law, the act of determining rights and assigning rewards or punishments. Peace is harmonious relations, free from violent disputes. Have the courage to stand for justice and to defend the peace.

12. Give Respect - John Wooden writes, "Never believe you're better than anybody else, but remember that you're just as good as everybody else." Treat others with dignity, respect, honesty and sensitivity. Encourage and practice teamwork. Appreciate that diversity is valuable. Diversity enables teams to create new ventures that are better than those created by a homogeneous (old boy) network.

13. Respect the Earth and Its Creatures - Think globally. Labor to achieve maximum results for all communities at minimum cost to the environment. Embrace sustainability.

14. **Walk the Talk -** Lead by example. Strive to stay true to your values in every action and communication. Use this yardstick: never say or do anything that you would not want your grandchildren to learn about when they come of age.

15. **Strive for Success -** Produce results that create value to realize your full potential and find fulfillment in your work. Success is within you. It's up to you to bring it out. Success comes from making the effort to become the best of which you are capable. Strive to improve a little each day, eventually big things will occur. Lasting success is not the big, quick improvement. Rather, it results from small improvements one day at a time. Success is not perfection. One can never reach perfection. Nevertheless, perfection is the goal.

Why Guiding Principles?

If you are an aspiring entrepreneur, you will find it helpful to view this question from two perspectives. First, look at it through the eyes of one who needs to become an extraordinary individual. Next, look at the question through the eyes of one who needs to build an extraordinary enterprise.

If you wish to be extraordinary, setting guiding principles will add clarity and purpose to your life. You know the results you are after. Your guiding principles explain why you want the results. They help keep you focused on what you must do to be extraordinary. Anthony Robbins argues that whatever you focus on in life tends to happen. He believes that life will pay whatever price you ask of it, but that you must ask intelligently. We offer you a link to a YouTube clip featuring Robbins. It is entitled "Clarity and Purpose." [1] Pay special attention to his RPM metaphor.

If you wish to build an extraordinary enterprise, consider the writings of Charles G. Koch. He sheds much light on the value of guiding principles in his book (2007), The Science of Success .[2] Koch is

[1, 2, 3] See 1-1 to 3 at
http://bit.ly/YourEntrepreneurialJourney

Chairman of the Board and CEO of Koch Industries, Inc. Koch Industries is possibly the largest privately-held collection of entrepreneurial business ventures in the world (annual revenues approximately $200 Billion). His book takes a holistic view of what it means to be an entrepreneur and what it takes to achieve venture success. We learned much from Koch's book and we strongly recommend it. The book is a "must read."

Koch considers guiding principles essential to entrepreneurial success. He coined the phrase "Principled Entrepreneurship" to give equal weight to both. To him, Principled Entrepreneurship means "maximizing long-term profitability for the venture by creating real value in society while always acting lawfully and with integrity." (Koch, p. 79) Koch believes, and we concur, that, to successfully do this, each venture, big or small, must *intentionally* create a culture with suitable, virtuous attributes. As Koch explains every venture "…has its own culture. It may be created intentionally by the… [venture] or inadvertently by other forces. In either case… [a venture's] culture is determined by the conduct of its members and the rules set by its leaders and governments." (Koch, p.79) We suspect that you will agree that inadvertently stumbling into the future is unlikely to lead to success.

For each new venture, success requires specific cultural attributes. Fortunately for Principled Entrepreneurs, they can: (1) identify the required, virtuous attributes for their venture, (2) describe them as Guiding Principles and (3) assure that all members of the venture team actively cultivate the Guiding Principles. As Koch says, these guiding principles "set the standards for evaluating policies and practices, measuring conduct, establishing norms of behavior and building the shared values that guide individual actions." (Koch, p. 80) Koch Industries, Inc. has eight guiding principles[3] Mihaylo Entrepreneurship has fifteen.

Being aware of your venture's necessary guiding principles is wise. Taking them to heart is wiser. However, developing the ability to apply your guiding principles routinely and instinctively to achieve results is wisest and best of all. Attaining this ability is critical to becoming a Principled Entrepreneur. Attainment is not easy, nor is it easy to stay in top form. Even highly skilled and accomplished entrepreneurs like Koch state that it requires constant practice and reflection. We agree. Mihaylo Entrepreneurship designed its learning experience to help you become a Principled Entrepreneur. Are you up to the challenge?

If you wish to be extraordinary, it's time to choose. Set your guiding principles and write them down. Explain each briefly in your own words. A rough draft is OK for now. The key is to write them down so they become apart of your Intellectual Property. Don't let your list gather dust. Refine the wording as you experience and learn.

22

Chapter 2: What are Guiding Principles, Really?

Compass Study **CC by 2.0** Calsidyrose

In this chapter, we explore what guiding principles really are, and what they are not.

Reading CFE's Fifteen Guiding Principles for the first time, one might conclude that they are very general and impractical. A skeptic might add that they only describe how to succeed in some sort of free-enterprise utopia.

Yes, our guiding principles are general. Assuredly, they are based on (1) our rules of just conduct, (2) our shared values and (3) our shared beliefs. However, far from being impractical, they face reality squarely. Practical experience and observation guide us rather than untested theories. Our guiding principles derive from our practical knowledge of what it takes to succeed.

Guiding principles give our stakeholders a solid foundation for making choices. With the right foundation, each of us can make great choices in any given situation we encounter. Rules, on the other hand, tell us what to do or not to do. In business, and in life, no two situations are alike. If we only tell our stakeholders what to do or not to do, how will they have the freedom to address new situations creatively? What if an old rule just doesn't apply to a new situation? When an ever-changing environment confronts us, guiding principles get us further. We know how to "be" and that helps us decide what to "do."

Mihaylo Entrepreneurship's guiding principles describe our "culture." They are the essence of our rules of just conduct, our shared values and our shared beliefs. Our culture is central to our success. The wise entrepreneur knows culture is important and lists the key elements for all involved in the venture.

For example, consider the words of Tony Hsieh, internet entrepreneur, venture capitalist and CEO of Zappos. He built Zappos' revenues from almost no sales to $1 billion in ten years. Hsieh explains the importance of culture and core values in a YouTube Video, "The Importance of a Company's Culture."[1] The website, zapposinsights.com, describes his firm's ten guiding principles as "Zappos 10 Core Values"[2] The website notes, "As we grow as a company, it has become more and more important to explicitly define the core values from which we develop our culture, our brand, and our business strategies." We list Zappo's ten core values here and recommend you visit the link provided in footnote 2-2 to read the clarification statements for each of the ten values:

1. Deliver WOW through Service
2. Embrace and Drive Change
3. Create Fun and A Little Wierdness
4. Be Adventurous, Creative and Open-Minded
5. Pursue Growth and Learning
6. Build Open and Honest Relationships with Communication
7. Build a Positive Team and Family Spirit
8. Do More With Less
9. Be Passionate and Determined
10. Be Humble

[1, 2, 3] See 2-1 to 3 at
http://bit.ly/YourEntrepreneurialJourney

For the leaders of entrepreneurial ventures, guiding principles are important tools. Carefully crafted by the venture's leaders, guiding principles work like a compass for all stakeholders. A compass points in the direction of "True North." However, it does not provide the roadmap. Similarly, guiding principles remind stakeholders about what is important. Wise, entrepreneurial leaders insist that all stakeholders stick to general, guiding principles. Simultaneously, they enable employees to challenge the particulars.

Guiding principles are not detailed rules or instructions. In entrepreneurial ventures, leaving the particulars to the people doing the work allows them to become principled entrepreneurs. (Koch, C. G. (2007) The Science of Success, p.79)[3] They have the flexibility to adapt to changing conditions and to be creative. They have the opportunity to maximize long-term profitability for the firm by creating real value in society, while always acting lawfully and with integrity. Over-specifying and enforcing rules lock people into the past. It undermines entrepreneurial growth and prosperity by encouraging people to be subservient and do nothing unless a rule tells them what to do.

To function effectively, your venture must have guiding principles that articulate your rules of just conduct along with your shared values and beliefs. However, general principles must largely guide your principled entrepreneurs, not specific commands. "Enforcing general principles enables employees to challenge the particulars. To the extent that particulars are enforced, the general breaks down." (Koch, p. 79)

You should try this: First Read Zappos core values, Koch Industries, Inc.'s guiding principles and Mihaylo Entrepreneurship's guiding principles (Chapter 1). Next, write the first draft of your own guiding principles for your venture. Craft the wording with the help of your stakeholders. Use your new compass to boost entrepreneurial growth and prosperity.

Chapter 3: What are the Requirements for Effective Use of Guiding Principles?

Pms XIII Coaching Clinic and Match **CC by 2.0**
Australian Government, Department of Foreign Affairs and Trade

In this Chapter, we explore two key requirements for effective use of guiding principles by entrepreneurs: leadership and coaching. If you do not consider yourself a leader and you dislike coaching, you are charting a course on troubled waters.

As an entrepreneur, you cannot do it all yourself. As your venture grows, you need to be a leader and get things done through others. Inevitably, the day will come when your people face tough decisions for you. You cannot be everywhere at once to make sure they all do the right thing. All you can do is prepare them well. At least well enough that they will come to the right conclusions by themselves.

The key question: How do you make sure that they do the right thing? How do you assure that everyone in the venture makes the right choices every day without requiring constant supervision?

Clayton Christensen, James Allworth and Karen Dillan tackle these questions in their book (2012) How Will You Measure Your Life? It is not as simple as distributing a list of guiding principles and hoping for the best. Something more fundamental has to occur and you have to do it.

In our view, if you aspire to be a successful leader, recognize that you will have to become a successful coach. This will require you to roll up your sleeves and work hard. Successful coaching requires that you consistently model and live by your venture's guiding principles – its rules of just conduct, shared values and shared beliefs.

[1,2,3,4] See 3-1 to 3-4 at
http://bit.ly/YourEntrepreneurialJourney

In addition, you must recognize that each of your people has different talents. How will you assess the talents? How will you develop each role player's talents and meld them into a successful team? Getting the answers is not a pen-and-paper exercise. You need to present your people with practical challenges. Assess how they respond. Repeatedly provide determined practice to develop their capabilities. It won't be easy for them or for you, but success is obtainable if you develop their virtues, talents and teamwork through determined practice.

To help you address your coaching challenge, Christensen et al. suggest that you employ the Resources, Processes, and Priorities model of capabilities. It will help you gauge what your people need. Following this model, each member of your team must become skilled at dealing individually and collaboratively with three elements: (1) the resources available, (2) the processes for accomplishing exceptional results, and (3) necessary priorities. Only through determined practice and shared learning will your people learn how to quickly evaluate their options and make good choices.

Benchmark your coaching skills against John Wooden, one of the most successful coaches in college basketball history. He summarized his guiding principles in his Pyramid of Success.[2] *Coach Wooden was a master at developing talent and teamwork. We offer you a link to his TED talk video, (2001)* "John Wooden: The difference between winning and succeeding" *in which he personally describes his pyramid of success.*[3] *Study his book (1988),* <u>They Call Me coach</u>.[4]

Chapter 4: How to Use Guiding Principles to Build Successful Ventures – Part One

Malala Yousafzai receives the European Parliament's Sakharov Human Rights Prize
CC by -ND 2.0 Edward McMillan-Scott MEP
emcmillanscott

*Our how-to discussion offers you three lessons: (1) What-it-is **is** what-it-is. (2) Do what must be done, and do it well. (3) Build teams first. In this chapter* *we present the first lesson. In Chapter five we will present the second and third lesson.*

The first lesson is, "What-it-is **is** what-it-is." Ours is not a perfect world. We strive for success in our personal life and our new ventures. Yet, life offers no guarantees. Our virtues, talents and teamwork do not guarantee venture success. Circumstances may overwhelm our strongest and most disciplined efforts – illness, injury, death, man-made calamities, natural disasters, and fierce, marketplace competition to name a few. We and our new ventures are born in a tough neighborhood.

We agree with Carol S. Dweck that the right "mindset" will help you thrive in our tough neighborhood. According to Dweck, our mindset frames the running account that's taking place in our heads. It guides the way we interpret what we see and how we respond. In her book (2006) Mindset: The New Psychology of Success, Dweck defines and contrasts two mind-sets: fixed and growth.[1] She summarizes her extensive research in a clever chart, (Dweck, p. 245), and on two websites: mindsetonline.com[2] and mindsetworks.[3]

[1, 2, 3, 4] See 4-1 to 4 at
http://bit.ly/YourEntrepreneurialJourney

One half of Dweck's chart describes the fixed mind-set. People with fixed mind-sets assume

"intelligence is static... [This] leads to a desire to look smart and therefore a tendency to... avoid challenges... get defensive ...[or] give up easily [when faced with challenges, they]... see effort as fruitless or worse... [dealing poorly with criticism they]... ignore useful negative feedback...[and finally, they] feel threatened by the success of others...As a result, they may plateau early and achieve less than their full potential." (Dweck, p.245) In our tough neighborhood, we believe people with fixed mindsets will likely fare much worse. They start by trying to look smart and many end as *victims*.

The other half of Dweck's Chart describes the growth mind-set. People with growth mind-sets assume "intelligence can be developed... [This] leads to a desire to learn and therefore a tendency to ... embrace challenges ... persist in the face of setbacks... see effort as the path to mastery... learn from criticism ...[and] find lessons and inspiration in the success of others... As a result, they reach ever-higher levels of achievement." (Dweck, p.245) We agree. People with growth mind-sets are *challengers*. If anyone can, they can survive and even thrive in our tough neighborhood.

Are you worried that you might not be up to the success challenge? Our advice to you is to TRY ANYWAY. Worrying about living in a tough neighborhood is OK. Being a bit paranoid about it is even OK. Still, the first lesson about how to use Guiding Principles to build successful ventures remains:"what-it-is, *is* what-it-is." Adopt Dweck's growth mind-set. Choose a worthwhile path. Take calculated risks to achieve what you believe must be done. Don't fear failure. Be confident in your ability to learn from setbacks and strengthen your capabilities. Be determined and persistent. Never give up. The "secret" to success is to be a challenger, not a victim.

Mere words cannot capture the self-discipline it takes to be a challenger. We offer you a link to a YouTube video that does. It is about motivation and discipline"[4]

You face many challenges. Ask yourself, "What would a victim do about them? What would a challenger do about them?" Choose to be a challenger. This choice is the key to success.

Chapter 5: How to Use Guiding Principles to Build Successful Ventures – Part two

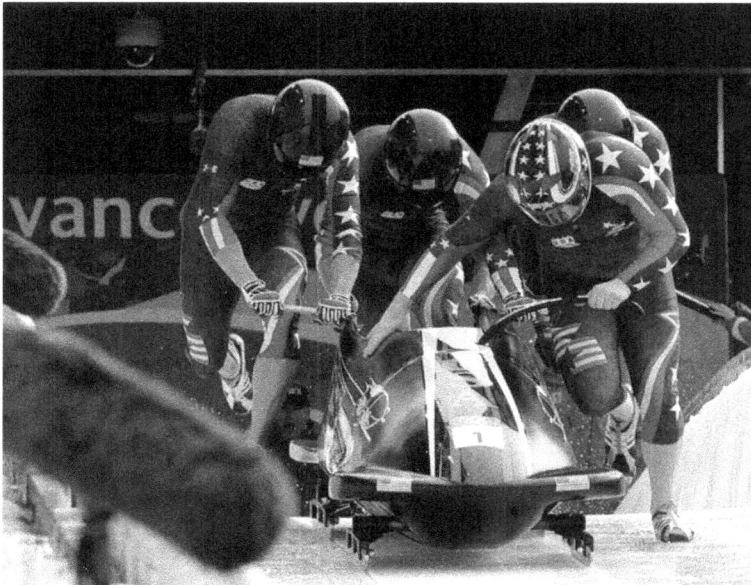

Former Army bobsledder helps win back-to-back Team of the Year awards **110125 CC by 2.0** U. S. Army familymwr

We continue our how to discussion that offers you three lessons: (1) What-it-is is what-it-is. (2) Do what must be done, and do it well. (3) Build teams first. Chapter 4 presented the first lesson. This chapter presents the second and third lesson.

The second lesson is, "do what must be done and do it well." We did not coin this lesson. Epictetus spoke about success in the early second century C.E., "First say to yourself what you would be; and then do what you have to do." Frequently, the popular press reports reaffirmations of this lesson. Many academic studies add support. For example, Dan Ariely argues that human motivation operates in far more complex ways than we understand. In his book, (2016) <u>Payoff: The Hidden Logic That Shapes Our Motivations</u>[1] Ariely explores how motivation works and how we can use this knowledge to build success for ourselves and others.

Success is raising yourself up to what you can be. Many religious thinkers believe that, if you never give up on this pursuit, you cannot fail. We offer you a link to a YouTube clip about Derek Redmond.[2] It shows that Mr. Redmond understands this lesson.

If you choose to strive for venture success, you will need to learn the answer to a key question: "Why do some companies thrive in our tough neighborhood and others do not?" Jim Collins and Morten T. Hansen explore this question in their book (2012)

[1, 2, 3, 4, 5] See 5-1 to 5 at
http://bit.ly/YourEntrepreneurialJourney

44

<u>Great by Choice</u>.[3] They conclude that "greatness is not primarily a matter of circumstance; greatness is first and foremost a matter of conscious choice and discipline. The factors that determine whether or not a company becomes truly great, even in a chaotic and uncertain world, lie largely within the hands of its people. It is not mainly a matter of what happens to them, but a matter of what they create, what they do, and how well they do it." (Collins and Hansen, p.182).

"Build teams first" is the third and final lesson on how to use Guiding Principles to build successful ventures.

In an earlier book, (2001) <u>Good to Great</u>, Jim Collins found that successful leaders followed the "First Who...Then What" principle.[4] Collins … "expected to find that the first step in taking a company from good to great would be to set a new direction, a new vision and strategy for the company, and then get people committed and aligned behind that new direction. [Instead he]... found that the executives who ignited the transformations from good to great did not first figure out where to drive the bus and then get people to take it there... They said in essence, 'Look, I don't really know where we should take this bus. But I know this much: If we get the right people on the bus, the right people in the right seats, and the wrong people off the bus, then we'll figure out how to take it someplace great.'" (Collins, p 41) "Build teams first" means that, first, you must understand the value of surrounding yourself with good people. Second, you must recruit people with leadership potential who share your guiding principles, whose talents complement yours.

Take an honest inventory of your strengths and weaknesses. Resist the temptation to recruit "yourself" to the team, meaning people you think are just like you. Instead, choose people with talents that complement yours and fill your "gaps." They will not crowd you out. Rather, they will become your competitive edge – the source of the extra intelligence, energy, and drive you need to accomplish great things.

Third, and conversely, you need to act quickly if one of your people is not a good fit. Perhaps, it turns out that the person does not share your vision and values. Perhaps, the person performs at a low level that puts you at a competitive disadvantage. In either case, you must take prompt corrective action. Since we know that no one is perfect, begin by attempting to improve the fit. Set focused strategies to help the person improve – training, development, mentoring or job change. However, if the person does not quickly respond to these efforts and continues to disappoint, you should not retain him or her. Invite the person to get off the bus.

Collins and Hansen make excellent points. However, we need to add that getting your top-flight team behind a new direction, a new vision or a new strategy requires determined practice. It takes more than handing out your brilliant business plan and directing them to make it happen.

Authority is certainly one way to influence, but not the best way to achieve peak results. To earn the best from your team, you need to intentionally create and consistently apply a communications experience - one that entertains, directs and inspires your team. Ben Decker and Kelly Decker explain how to do this in their book (2015) <u>Communicate to Influence: How to Inspire Your Audience to Action</u>.[5]

Revisit your guiding principles and what must be done. Are you frequently in the company of people who share your guiding principles? People whose talents complement yours and give your ventures a competitive edge?

Who will you invite on your bus? Where do you want them to sit? Who needs to get off the bus?

What is the communication experience that you offer? Does it entertain, direct and inspire?

Chapter 6: Create Value

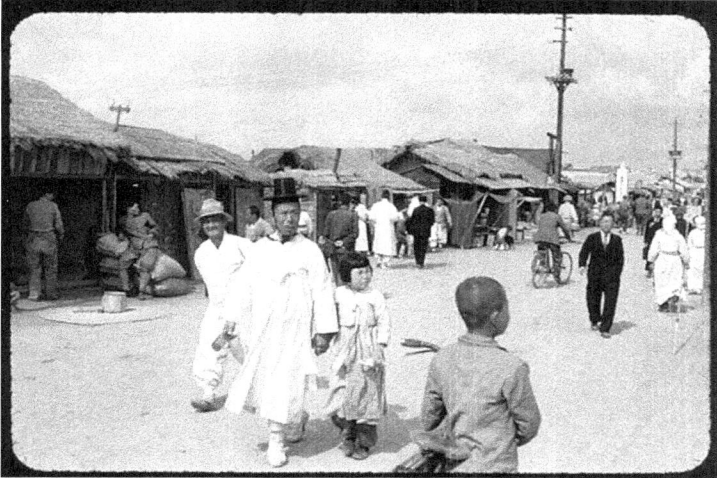

South of Seoul, South Korea (Local main street, circa 1952-53) **CC by 2.0** USAG-Humphreys

South of Seoul, South Korea (Busan, 2011) **CC by 2.0** Jirka Matousek

This chapter begins a principle-by-principle review of the CFE's Fifteen Guiding Principles with Principle One: Create Value. It explores how to create value in a market economy.

1. Create Value – Create real, long-term value by economic means. Understand, develop and apply entrepreneurial practices to achieve superior results for stakeholders and for the community. Eliminate excess, waste, and unevenness to achieve performance and cost effectiveness. Ensure excellence in environmental, safety, and all other areas of compliance – stop, think and ask.

What is the major take-away from our first Guiding Principle? We believe it is, "If you would be a successful entrepreneur, you must create real, long-term value by economic means." For profit or non-profit, your entrepreneurial ventures must create value for many, diverse stakeholders. Customers, suppliers, investors, employees and community, all must recognize that the venture achieves superior results.

Consider three questions: How do you do this? How do you create value by economic means? As an entrepreneur, what is your pathway to success in a market economy? To find answers you must first understand a basic truth -- *Only a small part of what you need to do will ever be under your direct command and control.*

To help you shape your answers to the above three questions, we offer four resources, two by entrepreneurs, and two by keen observers of what it takes to create value in a market economy. First is a video that highlights a successful entrepreneur's speech about entrepreneurial leadership. Second is an entrepreneur's book about creativity. Third, are excerpts from an article by a financial writer. Fourth is a book with a vision for the renewal of work in America.

First consider the speech. The presenter is Lance T. Shaner. He is Chairman and CEO of Shaner Hotel Group, L.P. After graduating from Alfred University, Mr. Shaner's entrepreneurial ventures started with a contract to rehab a bank-owned student housing project in 1988. At the time of the 2008 speech, the company owned and managed 60 hotels in 20 states. Brand affiliations include Marriott, Promus, Radisson, Holiday, Omni, and Embassy Suites. Mr. Shaner has served on the Board of Directors of United Way and the YMCA in State College, Pennsylvania. In the past he has been an advocate for disadvantaged children and worked in the development and construction of homes for lower income individuals. Lance is the father of three children, Sarah, Justin and Matt and has been married for over 30 years to his wife, Ellen. His ventures employ thousands and have assets exceeding $1 Billion. Mr. Shaner is not a vastly experienced, polished keynote speaker. However, his words are his own, and they come from the heart. In our experience, most successful entrepreneurs would applaud. We offer you a link to a YouTube summary of Mr. Shaner's 2008 speech about creating value in life and business.[1]

The second resource we offer is Edwin Catmull's book, (2014) <u>Creativity, Inc.: Overcoming the Unseen Forces That Stand in the Way of True Inspiration</u>.[2] Catmull is former president of Pixar and Walt Disney Animation Studios. As a computer scientist, he and creative teammates contributed many important developments in computer graphics and won multiple academy awards. His book is a thoughtful exploration of what it takes for innovative founders to create value for many, diverse stakeholders and "pivot" several times to achieve growth.

Now turn to the third resource we offer in this chapter. British financial writer John Kay provides insight into the value creation process and why much of the process is out of your control. In his

[1,2,3,4] See 6-1 to 4 at
http://bit.ly/YourEntrepreneurialJourney

article, (2009) "The Rationale of the Market Economy: A European Perspective,"[3] Kay argues that strong market economies have three components: (1) "Prices act as signals; the operation of the price mechanism is a better guide to resource allocation than central planning." (2) "Markets function as a process of discovery – the chaotic process of experimentation through which a market economy adapts to change." (3) "Markets yield benefits from the diffusion of political and economic power. Prosperity and growth require that entrepreneurial energy be focused on the creation of wealth rather than on the appropriation of other people's wealth." (Kay, p.1-2)

Kay coined the phrase, "economic pluralism" to weave these three components together. "When prices act as signals, decentralised enterprises and decentralised information are brought together to create a coherent result. Markets as a process of discovery are based on freedom to experiment, combined with discipline: unsuccessful experiment is acknowledged and terminated. Markets as a decentralising power illustrate how political and economic pluralism are closely associated in the achievement of an open society." (Kay, p.2)

Kay's discussion of "economic pluralism," provides a valuable perspective, especially the part about the need to focus entrepreneurial energy on the creation of wealth, rather than on the appropriation of other people's wealth. The fourth resource we offer in this chapter gives a broader perspective, "productive pluralism."

In many ways, studying economic pluralism is like watching 1950s network shows on a black- and-white TV with a rabbit-ear antenna. A wonder at the time. In contrast, exploring the implications of productive pluralism is like streaming today's favorite shows in high-definition color on a 65" flat-screen.

Oran Cass presents "productive pluralism" in his book (2018), The Once and Future Worker: A vision for the Renewal of Work in America.[4] For example, in his words, he "offers an alternative vision for long-term prosperity - rooted in the fact that productive pursuits – whether in the market, the community, or the family – give people purpose, enable meaningful and fulfilling lives, and provide the basis for strong families and communities that foster economic success too. Different people will accomplish this in different ways, so for this prosperity to be inclusive, it will need to accommodate numerous pathways, even at the expense of some efficiency." (Cass, p.6)

Self-evaluation: Write down your definition of yourself as an entrepreneur.

How does your definition compare to Lance Shaner's definition?

If you consider yourself to be an innovative founder, what will it take to create real, long-term value for many, diverse stakeholders? Are you prepared to "pivot" several times to do so?

Would John Kay say that your definition describes a wealth creator, or would he say it describes a wealth appropriator?

Will your ventures give your stakeholders purpose, enable meaningful and fulfilling lives, and provide the basis for strong families and communities?

Chapter 7: Embrace Change

Nautilus sp.Shell **CC by 2.0** Little Boffin (PeterEdin)

This chapter continues a Principle-by-Principle review of the CFE's Fifteen Guiding Principles with Principle Two: Embrace Change. In our view, the full meaning of embracing change encompasses much more than successfully pivoting a business model.

2. Embrace Change – Envision what could be, challenge the status quo and drive Joseph A. Shumpeter's "creative destruction," rather than being run over by it.

Many business models depict new-venture success as a two dimensional "J curve", or "hockey stick" curve. The J curve depicts cumulative cash flow. Initially, cumulative cash-flow is negative. Then, a positive turn around (still negative, but cumulatively some cash recovered). Finally, in a few time periods, free cash flow zooms linearly upwards. Graham Friend and Stefan Zehle authors of (2008) Guide to Business Planning[1], offer a clear description of the J curve.[2]

In reality, your pathway to success will be multi-dimensional and experimental. It will be unlike the linear progress of the two dimensional "J Curve".

In his book (2016) Smarter Faster Better: The Secrets of Being Productive in Life and Business[3], Charles Duhigg explains what it takes to challenge the status quo and embrace change. In his view, and most successful entrepreneurs would agree, productivity drives the real world "J" curve. Duhigg gets straight to the point on the front flap of his book cover, "Productivity relies on making certain choices. The way we frame our daily decisions; the big ambitions we embrace and the easy goals we ignore; the cultures we establish as leaders to drive

[1, 2, 3, 4, 5] See 7-1 to 5 at
http://bit.ly/YourEntrepreneurialJourney

innovation; the way we interact with data: these are the things that separate the merely busy from the genuinely productive."

No wonder that investors largely ignore the "J" curve in pitch decks and focus instead on the founding team. They ask themselves, do these people have what it takes to be genuinely productive? Will they be able to drive "creative destruction" in their industry rather than being run over by it?

Your pathway will be like an ocean voyage of discovery to an unknown, new continent. You will experience ever-changing weather conditions. Unexpected challenges will threaten to wreak your ship. To survive, you will have to make many course corrections. You will have to embrace change and stay genuinely productive.

To summarize, every pathway to success is difficult. You will need productivity skills to embrace change and successfully drive Shumpeter's creative destruction. As you attempt to focus your energies on next steps, imagining a J-shaped line on graph paper will not be an adequate map.

Instead, imagine that you are a chambered nautilis.[4] The chambered nautilis is an odd looking shellfish that carries its protective home on its back. It is a builder, building ever-larger living chambers as it grows.

Why is it beneficial to imagine that you must build - add to your shell - year after year? Oliver Wendell Holmes, Sr. says it best. His poem <u>The Chambered Nautilus</u> has many levels – just like success.[5]

The Chambered Nautilus

By <u>Oliver Wendell Holmes Sr.</u> 1809–1894
This is the ship of pearl, which, poets feign,
Sails the unshadowed main,—
The venturous bark that flings
On the sweet summer wind its purpled wings
In gulfs enchanted, where the Siren sings,
And coral reefs lie bare,
Where the cold sea-maids rise to sun their streaming hair.
Its webs of living gauze no more unfurl;
Wrecked is the ship of pearl!
And every chambered cell,
Where its dim dreaming life was wont to dwell,
As the frail tenant shaped his growing shell,
Before thee lies revealed,—
Its irised ceiling rent, its sunless crypt unsealed!
Year after year beheld the silent toil
That spread his lustrous coil;

Still, as the spiral grew,

He left the past year's dwelling for the new,

Stole with soft step its shining archway through,

Built up its idle door,

Stretched in his last-found home, and knew the old no more.

Thanks for the heavenly message brought by thee,

Child of the wandering sea,

Cast from her lap, forlorn!

From thy dead lips a clearer note is born

Than ever Triton blew from wreathed horn!

While on mine ear it rings,

Through the deep caves of thought I hear a voice that sings:—

Build thee more stately mansions, O my soul,

As the swift seasons roll!

Leave thy low-vaulted past!

Let each new temple, nobler than the last,

Shut thee from heaven with a dome more vast,

Till thou at length art free,

Leaving thine outgrown shell by life's unresting sea!

Use the Chambered Nautilus analogy to help you embrace change.

When should you start building the next chamber in your Nautilus Shell?

What should you change from the chamber where you now live?

Who will help with the build?

How can you be genuinely productive as you build?

Chapter 8: Apply Creativity

Walt Disney Concert Hall **CC by 2.0** Sheila Thomson
sheilaellen

*Principle Three is Apply Creativity. The two-word
summary of this principle may seem contradictory.
In reality, the words describe two solution "systems"
that reinforce each other. Used together, they yield
better, real-world solutions.*

3. Apply Creativity - Challenge conventional
approaches by applying curiosity, experimentation
and discovery to solve real world issues. Embrace
and encourage learning through hands-on, service-
based learning with dynamic, entrepreneurial
companies, and student startups.

What does it take for entrepreneurs to learn how to apply creativity? Application starts with discovery of a real world issue that "cries out" to you for solution.

Using creative tools like "brainstorming" you come up with a creative idea about how to tackle the issue. You believe your idea will work.

Your good idea compels you to finish what you started. By this we mean, you set your doubts and fears aside and vow to do whatever it takes to make it happen.

Then you go to work. We offer you a link to a YouTube clip entitled, "Best Motivational Video Ever for Creative People and Startups."[1] The clip shows, and we agree, that even getting to the starting line of the race is not easy. Once you do, *the race results will depend on your application skills.*

In many ways, when you launch a new venture you experience what a medical student experiences in medical school. The medical student must learn the application skills it takes to become a good doctor. You must learn the application skills it takes to be a successful entrepreneur.

[1, 2, 3] See 8-1 to 8-3 at
http://bit.ly/YourEntrepreneurialJourney

Getting accepted into medical school is a major accomplishment. However, the learning has just begun. What do top medical schools do to transform students into good doctors? How do they transform the students into MDs who are experts at applying creativity? The faculty employ a tutorial process. The process teaches a "solution "system" for diagnosing and treating patients.

Howard S. Barrows' book describes the tutorial process used in medical schools, (1988) The Tutorial Process.[2] After years of systematic training, medical students must still get practical clinical experience through guided practice.

Experts tutor the students, directing the development of the students' reasoning skills as they work with ill-structured problems. The students learn how to critique the adequacy of their work, and how to direct their own continuing learning.

In short, with the help of their tutors, they learn how to apply creativity. (Barrows, p. 3) As an entrepreneur, you need to learn a similar application approach and apply them to your venture. The big difference is that, in most cases, you must find your own experts to tutor you.

Daniel Kahneman is a winner of the Nobel Prize in economics. Kahneman's book, (2011) <u>Thinking, Fast and Slow</u>, [3] adds additional insights concerning Principle 3 -- Apply Creativity.

He argues that, within us, two "systems" drive the way we think. System 1, is fast, intuitive and emotional. System 2 is slower, more deliberative and more logical. As entrepreneurs, we might say that System 1 describes our creative side, and System 2 describes our applied side. Within us, each system has its individual abilities, limitations and functions. Kahneman explores them in depth.

Early in his book, Kahneman, points out that, "we identify with System 2, the conscious reasoning self that has beliefs, makes choices, and decides what to think about and what to do. Although System 2 believes itself to be where the action is, the automatic System 1 is the hero of the book. I describe System 1 as effortlessly originating impressions and feelings that are the main sources of the explicit beliefs and deliberate choices of System 2." (Kahneman, p. 21)

On the other hand don't discount the value of System 2. As Kahneman says "Only the slower System 2 can construct thoughts in an orderly series of steps. [Sometimes it]... takes over,

70

overruling the freewheeling impulses and associations of System 1." (Kahneman, p. 21)

Riding a spirited idea (System 1) is like riding a spirited horse. It is wise not to unbridle your creativity and try to ride bareback until you become a competent rider.

Whether you are a horseback rider, a medical student, or an aspiring entrepreneur, it takes many years of guided practice to develop unconscious competence. Until then, and even beyond, you will find the ride smoother if you apply the bridle and saddle (System 2).

When embarking on new ventures, and dealing with ill-structured business problems along the way, you are the "MD." Do you want to hone your ability to apply creativity? Get started by using The Medical School Method.

The Medical School Method
1. Develop an **initial concept** of the problem based on information available at the outset.
2. Generate **multiple hypotheses** as to the cause of the problem.
3. Carry out an appropriate **inquiry** to attempt to establish the more likely cause.
4. **Analyze** new data obtained through inquiry as it relates to the forming picture of the problem.
5. Add the new data thought to be significant, particularly in the light of the hypotheses obtained, to a growing **problem synthesis**.
6. **Continue** this process, scanning for new information when stuck, creating new hypotheses as appropriate.
7. **Decide** at an appropriate point, despite inadequate or confusing data, on the most logical cause (hypothesis) and the appropriate treatment for the problem using criteria such as prevalence, seriousness, and treatability.
8. **Treat** the problem.
9. **Review based on reactions.**

Think like a MD and you will find better solutions to your venture's problems!

-

Chapter 9: Celebrate Uniqueness

"Always remember that you are absolutely unique. Just like everyone else."
~ Margaret Mead

You are unique **CC by 2.0** Celestine Chua

Principle Four is Celebrate Uniqueness. Uniqueness is multidimensional and malleable. As you grow, you can shape your uniqueness, and reshape it, to suit your purpose. If your purpose is worthwhile, it will add value to your culture or community. Adding value will attract resources and allow you to increase value.

4. Celebrate Uniqueness - Each of us has a special purpose in life and it is no accident that we are on this planet. Each of us has unique skills. It is your responsibility to discover your purpose and to do your best to fulfill it by developing and employing your skills.

In our view, no one defines your uniqueness at birth. You are not born with a certain amount of uniqueness. Uniqueness is multidimensional and malleable. In life many good and bad things will happen to you. As you grow, you can shape your uniqueness, and reshape it, to suit your purpose. If your purpose is worthwhile, it will add value to your culture or community, attract resources and allow you to add more value. As you strive to accomplish your purpose, to add value, you will earn a sense of accomplishment, self-respect and the respect of others.

Consider two entrepreneurs, each unique. They differ in many ways, but they are alike in the passionate pursuit of their purpose throughout their careers. First we offer you a link to a short YouTube clip entitled, "Steve Jobs' Advice for Entrepreneurs."[1] Jobs, the founder of Apple, makes the point that you have to have passion for your purpose. Unless you do, you can't sustain the hard work needed to succeed.

Second, we introduce you to Adam Leipzig, CEO Entertainment Media Partners. He has been involved as a producer, distributor or supervising

[1, 2, 3] See 9-1 to 9-3 at
http://bit.ly/YourEntrepreneurialJourney

executive on more than 25 films that have disrupted expectations, including March of the Penguins, Honey, I Shrunk the Kids, and "Dead Poets Society.

Leipzig's movies have produced over $2 billion in revenue with less than $300 million in production investment. He has twice been responsible for the "most profitable film of the year"

Leipzig's films have won or been nominated for 10 Academy Awards, 11 BAFTA Awards, 2 Golden Globes, 2 Emmys, 2 Directors Guild Awards, 4 Sundance Awards and 4 Independent Spirit Awards. We offer you a link to a YouTube clip featuring Mr. Leipzig. It is entitled, "How to Know Your Life Purpose in 5 Minutes."[2]

Leipzig lists five questions you must answer to learn your life purpose:
1. Who are you?
2. What do you do?
3. Who do you do it for?
4. What do they want or need?
5. How do they change or transform as a result of what you give them?

Key to Leipzig's list is that only the first two questions are inward facing. The other three are outward facing.

Let's assume your passion for your purpose is burning bright. What makes you unique? How do you shape your uniqueness, and reshape it, to suit your purpose?

Howard Gardner explores part of what we mean by uniqueness in his book (2004) <u>Changing Minds</u>.[3] Gardner defines intelligence and provides a provisional list of multiple intelligences, e.g., linguistic, mathematical, spatial, bodily-kinesthetic and so on.

Gardner's intelligence definition is, "a biopsychological potential to process specific forms of information in certain kinds of ways. Human beings have evolved diverse information-processing capacities – I term these 'intelligences' – that allow them to solve problems or to fashion products. To be considered 'intelligent' these products and solutions must be valued in at least one culture or community." (Gardner, p.29)

Despite the richness of this scholarly definition, your special mix of "intelligences" does not clearly define what we mean here by uniqueness. We add two clarifications.

First, as Gardner recognizes, "human beings value different skills and capacities at various times and under varying circumstances." (Gardner, p.30) What this means is that both your purpose and uniqueness must evolve.

Otherwise you will not remain valuable to society throughout your life. You will not be able to serve changes in peoples core needs. As you evolve, you must stay on point. You must avoid pandering to superficial wants.

The second clarification is that the physical assets and people you enlist to your purpose *fall within your sphere of influence*. Their value, purpose and uniqueness become aligned with yours. They voluntarily channel their energy to help you build, enhancing your skills and your capacity to get things done.

For example, years ago a young friend of ours formed a successful landscape company called Edible Landscape. His purpose, "design and build home food gardens that are sustainable and artfully arranged." His garden designs were beautiful, nutritious and easy to maintain. His purpose and the uniqueness of his designs, attracted loyal employees and clientele. Our friend was a quadriplegic.

He could not do the physical work in the office or in the field. He *had* to employ his purpose and uniqueness to enlist customers, employees and suppliers to help him build a successful venture.

How would you answer Leipzig's five, life-purpose questions?

1. Who are you?
2. What do you do?
3. Who do you do it for?
4. What do they want or need?
5. How do they change or transform as a result of what you give them?

Write down your answers and act immediately on your findings. Remember, as Leipzig relates in his YouTube clip, the unexamined life is not worth living, but if you spend all your time examining, you are not living.

Chapter 10: Build Community

Habitat-for-Humanity-81 **CC by 2.0** First Baptist Nashville FirstBaptistNashville

Principle Five is Build Community. We assert that a link exists between your purpose and building community. Your success derives from virtuous cycles driven by your worthwhile purposes and your work to build community. Developing this viewpoint is important. We derive maximum success from creating maximum value at minimum cost. This chapter provides four examples.

5. Build Community – No entrepreneur has ever succeeded on his/her own. Find out what people need. Study larger community concerns. Make people's lives better while consuming fewer resources, leaving more resources available to satisfy other community needs. Certainly, reward your people according to the value they create for the venture. However, do not forget to also reward them for resource conservation and renewal.

In our previous discussion of Principle Four: Celebrate Uniqueness, we asserted two things. First, it is your responsibility to discover your purpose and to do your best to fulfill it. Second, if your purpose is worthwhile, it will add value to your culture or community, attract resources and allow you to add more value. (Chapter 9)

In other words, we assert that a link exists between your purpose and building community. Your success derives from virtuous cycles driven by your worthwhile purposes and your work to build community. Developing this viewpoint is important. We derive maximum success from creating maximum value *at minimum cost*. What are the implications? Consider four examples. First, we offer you a link to a thought-provoking YouTube Video (2017) "Finding Your Purpose in Life and Living Your Dream."[1] The video is an interview

[1, 2, 3, 4, 5] See 10-1 to 5 at
http://bit.ly/YourEntrepreneurialJourney

with Oprah Winfrey at the Stanford Graduate School of Business.

Winfrey stresses that she lives "from inside out." In her view, your intentions will determine your actions and the results or consequences. She feels that her "calling" is to help people improve their lives.

Accordingly, Winfrey often asks herself if her intentions are true to her calling. At work, she asks herself and her producers if the intentions of the show's proposed content are true to the calling of the show's platform. Winfrey wants her show to bring positive change the world. To do so, she argues, you must help people to connect themselves to higher levels of consciousness (*their* callings). She believes her show's success comes from helping people make these connections.

Consider a second example of the links between your purpose and building community. In his book (2003) Good Business[2], Mihaly Csikszentmihalyi argues that "there are many successful, law-abiding business leaders who in private life are thoughtful and generous, but who do not regard taking responsibility for more than profits as part of their job." (Csikszentmihalyi, p.209) Their viewpoint is that they and their ventures compete *against* the world. How much more successful might they be if, instead, their viewpoint was: we and our ventures work *for* the world?

Turning to a third example, Third, Peter J. Denning and Robert Dunham, in their book (2010), <u>The Innovator's Way</u>[3], point out that Google and W3C "are examples of organizations that rely on a dispersed network to help them innovate. The W3C is a consortium of diverse organizations from many industry sectors. Google manages an ecosystem of content providers, advertisers, consumers, and innovators. Both have successfully created vast learning networks." (Denning & Dunham, p.306). Today, change in global communities is much faster and less predictable. It appears that Google and W3C have the viewpoint that innovation is learning how to succeed in this environment. In this context, their learning networks are not simply information sharing or surveillance networks. They are a community of people learning practices from each other. (Denning & Dunham, p.306)

Finally, a fourth example. According to Trends Magazine, over the next several decades, global economic growth faces a serious threat: a catastrophic shortage of natural resources, which have become increasingly hard to find and extract. (Trends Magazine, September, 2012, p.10)[4] Which viewpoint will prove more successful? The viewpoint that value creation is a linear economic process: Take natural resources - make something useful - dispose of the obsolete or worn-out product. Or, the viewpoint that value creation must be a virtuous cycle - successful producers and consumers must build communities that both maximize value and minimize costs. They do this by designing for reclaimation and improvement - recycling valuable learning, materials and components back into ever more efficient and effective production.

We offer you a challenge. Trends Magazine reports that, on average, we can extract only five grams of gold from a ton of ore taken from a gold mine. In contrast, we could extract up to 150 grams of gold from a ton of discarded mobile phones (not to mention the value of the rare-earth minerals employed in cell phones). (Trends, September 2012, p. 11.)[5] What kind of community would you need to build in order to profitably extract gold and other rare earth minerals from discarded cell phones?

Chapter 11: Maintain Personal Integrity and Trust

Love and trust – father tosses his confident daughter into the air accompanied by screams of delight **CC by 2.0** Mike Baird mikebaird

Principle Six is Maintain Personal Integrity and Trust. Keeping your promises and being reliable leads to success. Personal integrity and trust are also leadership issues. People know and follow the "real deal" when they see it -- the leaders who walk through life on their own terms, who stay true to their beliefs, and exhibit a can-do spirit when times get tough.

6. Maintain Personal Integrity and Trust - Keep the promises you make to others and to yourself. Be the person that others can rely upon and place confidence in, both in good times and bad.

Keeping your promises and being reliable leads to success. How does this happen? David Novak is retired Chairman and CEO of Yum! Brands, Inc., by some measures the world's largest restaurant company with brands like KFC, Pizza Hut and Taco Bell. After he retired in 2016, he became Founder and CEO of oGoLead, a digital leadership development platform created to help people become better leaders by teaching vital Heartwiring™ and Hardwiring™ skills.

In his book, (2012) Taking People With You: The Only Way to Make BIG Things Happen,[1] Novak argues that your ability to reach your BIG goals relates to how you choose to view the world.

Following Novak's thinking, effective leadership has two preconditions. First, to be the one who builds

[1,2,3] See 11-1 to 3 at
http://bit.ly/YourEntrepreneurialJourney

the "best" community, you must begin by building your "best" self. You must be trustworthy and authentic even in the toughest situations. In Novak's view, people know and follow the "real deal" when they see it: the leaders who walk through life on their own terms, who stay true to their beliefs, and don't back down.

Second, to cultivate the can-do spirit in those around you, you first need to cultivate the can-do spirit in yourself. You have to expect to win through hard work, preparation, and adaptability. You need to know your stuff, but you also must admit when you don't know stuff. In short, you need to be confident enough to confront challenges and humble enough to always be learning.

What does learning have to do with integrity? We offer you a book and two short stories to think about.

Many years ago, so the first story goes, the struggling young founder of a startup venture learned a life-changing lesson on a short commuter flight. The youngster, an avid reader, had three books in her briefcase. She selected one by a renowned industry leader, 30 years her senior.

As she opened the dog-eared book, her seat mate arrived. None other than the author of the book. A friendly conversation followed. Encouraged, the youngster asked, "Which chapter in your book contains the lesson most important to your success?" The author smiled. She said, "The one about integrity and wisdom."

A bit confused, the youngster asked, "What is the difference between integrity and wisdom?"

She replied, "Integrity means keeping your promises, even if you go bankrupt.
Wisdom comes from learning not to make such promises."

For too many entrepreneurs, the need to practice this story's definition of wisdom becomes a harsh reality. Ventures fail when startup ambitions outpace finances. Personal integrity and investor trust hinge on financial discipline.

Mike Michalowicz describes how he lost both integrity and trust in his book, (2017) Profit First: Transform Your Business from a Cash-Eating Monster to a Money Making Machine [2] He also shares how he recaptured integrity and trust by learning to be a better money manager. It was a long hard road. Now Michalowiz knows to consistently base his financial decisions on what his ventures need, rather than on what he thinks he wants. He is on the path to wisdom.

The second short story may be found on YouTube. We offer you, "Life is Like a Cup of Coffee."[3]

Think about the high and low points in your life. How did each high and low relate to your ability to maintain your personal integrity and the trust of others? How did each high and low relate to your focus – coffee or cup?

Chapter 12: Be Aware of Right and Wrong

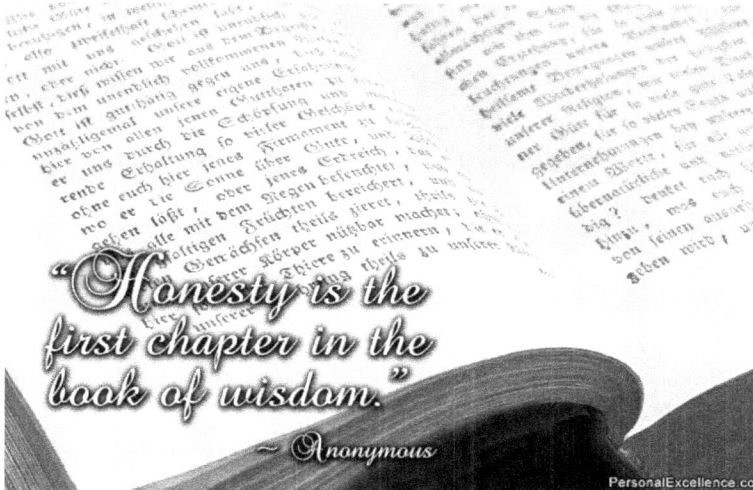

"Honesty is the first chapter in the book of wisdom."

~ Anonymous

Honesty **CC by 2.0** Celestine Chua

Principle Seven is: Be Aware of Right and Wrong. We strongly word Principle Seven. This chapter introduces two key questions to help you understand why. In your lifetime, faced with life's dilemmas, you will experience thousands of variations of these two questions. To be successful, you will need to answer them well nearly always and act accordingly.

7. Be Aware of Right and Wrong – Do good. Never lie, never cheat, never steal. Conduct all affairs lawfully and with integrity. Everyone deserves to be treated fairly.

The word "never" is a strong word to include in the description of a guiding principle. Yet it appears three times here. So do the words "all" and "everyone." Strong wording leads to two key questions: (1) Why is constant awareness of right and wrong so essential? (2) Why is it so imperative for each step you take to be right, good, legal and fair?

In your lifetime, you will experience thousands of variations of these two questions. Over the centuries, untold millions of successful people have answered them well nearly always. Likewise, millions of unsuccessful people have answered them well most of the time. Learn from the successful. We suspect that they would underscore the words "never," "all," and "everyone." Success is not perfection. One can never reach perfection. Nevertheless, perfection is the goal. The pathway to success is a long one. You can choose the wrong answer a few times and still succeed. However, you must act quickly and pay the price (often high) for your misstep. Learn and do what must be done to get back on your pathway to success.

C. S. Lewis said, "The safest road to Hell is the gradual one - the gentle slope, soft underfoot, without sudden turnings, without milestones, without signposts." Many contemporary business writers echo this theme. For example, in Section III of his book (2012) <u>How Will You Measure Your Life</u>?[1], Clayton Christensen builds on C. S. Lewis' words. Appropriately, Section III is entitled, "Staying Out of Jail." (Christensen, pp. 175-206.)

We offer you two resources that provide insights about the practical meaning of Principle Seven. The first resource is a speech by Mary Brainerd. She was President and CEO of HealthPartners for fifteen years until her retirement in 2017. HealthPartners is the largest consumer governed nonprofit health care organization in the nation with over 20,000 employees. The title of her 2014 speech (2014) is, "The Return on Integrity: Ethics, Values and Business."[2] Ms. Brainerd uses W. Clement Stone's definition of integrity as the starting point for her presentation, "The courage to say no. The courage to face the truth. The courage to do the right thing because it is right."

The second resource we offer you is a short-story. The dilemma it presents illustrates how difficult staying on your path to success is.

[1, 2] See 12-1 to 2 at
http://bit.ly/YourEntrepreneurialJourney

The real estate market was on the upswing and Ken had learned handy man skills from his dad. His approach to real estate investing was simple: use other people's money to buy a home, beautify it, sell it "as is" and split the profits with his investors. (One calls this process "flipping.")

Initially, Ken's investors were family and friends. He kept a little black book. In it, he recorded the name of each investor, the amount invested, and left space to enter the profits they would earn. Ken, budgeted his money carefully, worked hard and made his investors money in short order. Impressed, they reinvested. As his track record developed, friends of friends heard about him and offered to invest. Pleased, he added them to his little black book. Also, a local bank granted Ken a generous line of credit. To put the new money to work, he formed crews of subcontractors and began working with real estate agents to find properties. Soon, he had ten homes flipping at once, then twenty, then thirty. Things went well for two years. Then Ken's worries mounted.

He began to feel a profit-squeeze. Acquisition costs for fixer-uppers kept rising and the available properties needed more work. Repair costs rose and the time it took to flip properties slowed as buyers had a harder time financing Ken's asking prices. Soon, his line of credit was fully drawn. He owed the bank several hundred thousand dollars. Fortunately, based on his track record, the bank did not demand repayment of the principal when it was due. Instead, it allowed him to "roll over" the principal for a few more months and pay interest only on the balance due.

Despite Ken's policy of selling property "as is," buyers increasingly complained about significant defects they claimed were undisclosed at the time of purchase. Ken fixed what he could, but soon faced lawsuit threats.

Profit entries in Ken's little black book approached zero. Investors became concerned. Some felt cheated and wanted their money back.

Adding to his worries, Ken heard rumors that the housing market was going to get worse. Shortly before the housing bubble burst, he tried to sell his properties. Many were in the middle of repairs. Only a few properties sold. Ken asked the bank to roll over his line of credit again. The bank refused and demanded full repayment of the principal. Ken felt he was up against the wall and the firing squad was taking aim.

If you were Ken, what would you do?

Write your own short-story describing a dilemma that you face. Ask people you know and trust to read it and describe what they would do. How well do their proposed actions answer the two key questions in this chapter?

Chapter 13: Love Learning, Wisdom and Truth

Life is about learning to dance in the rain **CC BY-SA 2.0** SEO FindYourSearch

Principle Eight is Love Learning, Wisdom and Truth. In this chapter, we argue that, as an entrepreneur, you begin well if you have great ideas and entrepreneurial spirit. However, you will not go far if you do not acquire needed resources and manage them expertly to produce real value. The most productive resource you have is your venture's "brain." You must manage its development. The key to doing so is to love learning, wisdom and truth.

8. Love Learning, Wisdom and Truth – Have the courage to kindle your desire to learn. Find lessons and inspiration in the success of others. As Charles Koch writes, "seek and use the best knowledge and proactively share your knowledge while embracing a challenge process. Measure profitability where practical." Adopt the elements of Carol Dweck's growth mind-set. Your greatest power is free-will. You possess the power of choice. For any endeavor, choose to develop your intelligence through determined practice aided by selection of good coaches. Effort is the path to mastery. Embrace challenges and persist in the face of setbacks. Most all good things come through adversity.

Sixty-five years ago, Peter Drucker published (1954) The Practice of Management. (2006 reprint currently available from HarperCollins Publishers, Inc. Business)[1] Some say this classic work was the first to look at management as a distinct function, managing as specific work, and being a manager as a separate responsibility. As an entrepreneur, you begin well if you have great ideas and entre- preneurial spirit. However, you will not go far if you do not acquire needed resources and manage them

[1, 2] See 13-1 to 2 at
http://bit.ly/YourEntrepreneurialJourney

expertly to produce real value. In Drucker's words, "The enterprise must control wealth-producing resources to discharge its purpose..." (Drucker, p.41) Your management responsibility is to use these resources productively. "Productivity means that balance between *all* factors of production that will give the greatest output for the smallest effort." (Drucker, p. 41) We might add that, if you mismanage the resources entrusted to you, you will lose the right to control them.

Achieving the right balance of factors is essential for your success. However, not all factors are equally important. According to Drucker, "The basic factor in an economy's development must be the rate of 'brain formation,' the rate at which a country produces people with imagination and vision, education, theoretical and analytical skill." (Drucker, p.42) The same holds true for your venture. The most productive resource you have, the most important one for you to develop, is your venture's "brain" - your team of managers, planners, designers, and innovators.

In short, you are the manager of "brain formation" for yourself and your venture. Increasing the rate of brain formation is your responsibility and is essential for your success. The key to increasing the rate of brain formation is to love learning, wisdom and truth. Often the path to learning wisdom and truth is incredibly hard. One must possess a growth mindset, and a determined personality that loves the challenge.

Consider the path followed by Ramona Pierson. Pierson first learned to write computer code in the U. S. Marine Corps. In recent years, she founded SynapticMash, an education software company she sold to Promethean World for a reported $10 million in 2010. Her second startup evolved into a big-data platform known as Declara, Inc. Officially launched in May 2013, the company's initial aim was to help teachers create more personalized lessons for students. Declara is now an artificial intelligence enabled social learning platform for Innovation and human capital development. Pierson remains Chairman and CEO of Declara, Inc. In 2017 she joined Amazon as Head of Learning Products. She is currently Director of Product Management at Amazon.

What is inspiring is the incredibly hard path to learning, wisdom and truth that Pierson faced, yet chose to follow. In the resource folder, click on the YouTube link to hear her describe it in her own words. Her talk is entitled, "Learning to Learn."[2]

Are you facing a big challenge and not sure where to start? Try using a simple learning tool that we call a Knowledge Sheet. At the top of a sheet of note book paper briefly describe your challenge. Divide the rest of the sheet into three columns of equal width. Write "What I Know" at the top of the left column. Next, write "What I Need to Know" at the top of the middle column. Finally, write "How I will Find Out" at the top of the right column.

Begin filling the columns by writing what you know in the left column. As you see gaps in your knowledge, write what you need to know in the middle column. Continue until you have a good feel for what you know and what you need to know. Next, move to the right column and write how you will find out what you need to know.

Advanced tip: Want ideas from your entire team? Bring them together. Give them blank Knowledge Sheets with the challenge description at the top. Take 10-15 quiet minutes to have each team member independently fill the three columns on his/her sheet. When done, compare notes and write a combined Knowledge Sheet for the entire team.

Chapter 14: Practice Humility and Intellectual Honesty

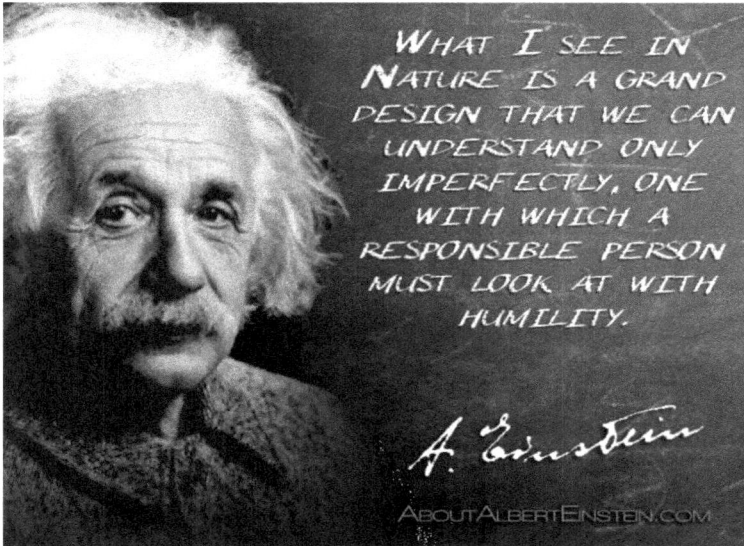

What I see in Nature is a grand design that we can understand only imperfectly, one with which a responsible person must look at with humility. **CC by 2.0** QuotesEverlasting. (Also credits AboutAlbertEinstein.com)

Principle Nine is Practice Humility and Intellectual Honesty. Far from theory, this principle is hard-nosed, common sense. It is about how to decide, and improve your chances for success, in a rapidly changing world. In this chapter we discuss three methods that help us to practice humility and intellectual honesty.

9. Practice Humility and Intellectual Honesty - Constantly seek to understand and constructively deal with reality to create real value and achieve personal improvement. Actively seek criticism and learn from it. Don't whine, don't complain, and don't make excuses

Kevin J.Murphy, in his book (1987) <u>Effective Listening</u>[1], observes that one's ego is the most basic block to effective listening. "By providing each of us with an enormous need to be *heard*, our egos overwhelm any desire to *hear*. An open mind is the key to communication." (Murphy, pp.13-14.)

In our view, Murphy's observation applies to all forms of communication. When our ego gets in the way, our "entrepreneurial spirit" overwhelms our common sense. Heart overwhelms head. Reality becomes hard to discover and constructive response is unlikely. If you are occasionally tempted to think your new venture is the center of the universe, (and we all are!), click the following link and view the YouTube clip. It puts ego in place and opens the mind. The clip is entitled, "Star Size Comparison."[2]

[1, 2, 3, 4, 5] See 14-1 to 5
http://bit.ly/YourEntrepreneurialJourney

In a conventional world, with stable technologies and an established customer base, an entrepreneur's strong ego might help push things forward. The entrepreneur's focused, dogged, adherence to his/her grand plan might work. If so, credit another victory to the power of the entrepreneurial spirit.

However, in an unconventional world where technologies and customers are untested, failure is far more likely. Entrepreneurs build preconceived business plans on *assumptions* rather than *facts*. If the entrepreneur does not practice humility and intellectual honesty, the entrepreneur's ego will dismiss reality. Mistaken, unchallenged assumptions will kill the venture. If several founders bring their unbridled egos to the table, extinction will occur even faster.

Rita Gunther McGrath and Ian C. MacMillan recommend a common sense method that will help you harness the team of egos that drive your enterprise. They call it discovery driven planning (1995[3], 1999[4]). Here, we offer a quotation from their 1999 discussion, "Discovery Driven Planning: Turning Conventional Planning on its Head".

 "The core premise behind discovery driven planning is that companies need to be able to plan in such a way that expenses are minimized and learning is maximized. Rather than asking whether managers met projections, a discovery orientation asks whether they managed expenditures with discipline, whether they were conscious about the assumptions they were making, and whether they exhausted all possible ways to create new knowledge before making irreversible commitments. The whole idea, in other words is to project as far, but not farther, than is sensible given existing knowledge... Unless you are very disciplined about documenting and testing your assumptions, you are likely to become a victim to the single greatest problem to beset new business organizations, namely the treatment of assumptions as facts." (p. 2)

What if you make a mistake? How will you recover? Adam Bryant in his book (2011) The Corner Office[5], includes words from an interview with Jen-Hsun Huang of Nvidia. Huang argues that "learning from failure, and recognizing failure quickly"... is an important part of any company that's in a rapidly changing world
... [You need to practice]
intellectual honesty – the ability to call a spade a spade, to recognize as quickly as possible that we've made a mistake, that we've gone the wrong way, and that we learn from it and quickly adjust."

(Bryant, pp.34-35)

Methods such as Effective Listening, Discovery Driven Planning, and Learning from Failure help us to practice humility and intellectual honesty. What has to prove true for your venture to succeed? What methods can you use to assure that you have tempered (and strengthened) your dreams of success by your understanding of reality?

Chapter 15: Be Caring and Compassionate

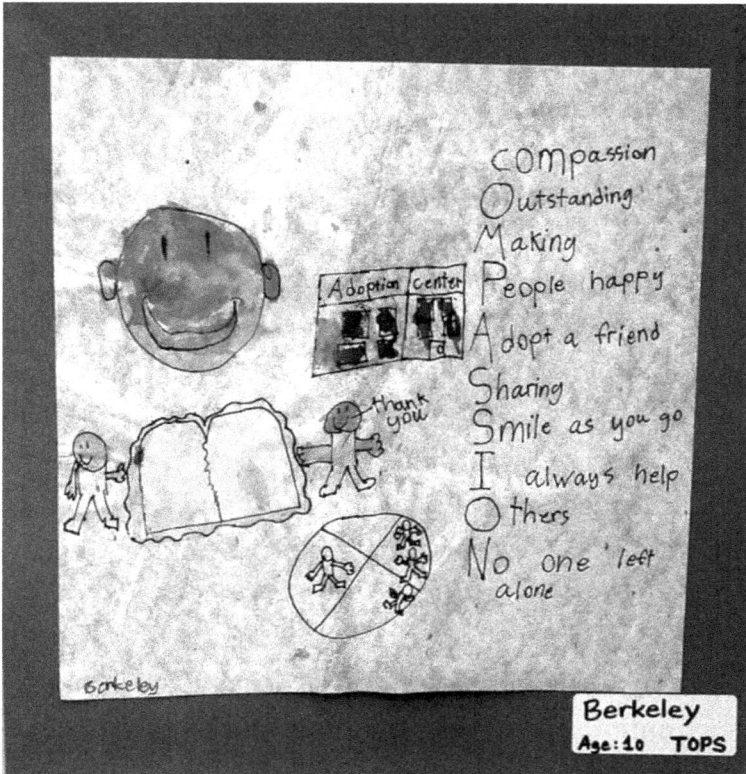

Compassion Outstanding Making People happy Adopt a friend Sharing Smile as you go I always help Others No one left alone, Berkeley, Age 10, TOPS, Seattle, Library, University of Washington, USA **CC by 2.0** Wonderlane

Principle Ten is Be Caring and Compassionate.
Caring and compassion are essential elements of
the human side of enterprise. Revenues from these
"soft" elements do not appear on income

statements. However, being caring and compassionate positively influences sustained profitability. More importantly, caring and compassion contribute to personal fulfillment, meaningful enterprise purpose and social improvement.

10. Be Caring and Compassionate – Principled entrepreneurs succeed by helping others to succeed. You cannot live a perfect day without doing something for another without thought of something in return. Give to others unconditionally.

What does being caring and compassionate have to do with success? The words caring and compassion do not often appear in popular biographies of entrepreneurs. Nor do the words caring and compassion often appear in the writings of respected, business-strategy experts. Still, in our view, caring and compassion are essential elements of the human side of enterprise.

John Wooden, writing with Steve Jamison in (1997) <u>Wooden: A Lifetime of Observations and Reflections On and Off the Court</u>[1], defines success as "peace of mind which is a direct result of self-

1, 2, 3, 4, 5, 6, 7, 8, 9, 10, 11, 12, 13 See 15-1 to 13 at
http://bit.ly/YourEntrepreneurialJourney

satisfaction in knowing that you did your best to become the best that you are capable of becoming."(Wooden & Jamison, p. 174) How can we claim to be successful, if we limit our definition of success to personal wealth accumulation or corporate profit maximization? How can we be satisfied with winning solely in economic terms? The free enterprise system works because it is much more than the rules of the game for a money race. It opens opportunities for all to earn self-fulfillment.

In this context, founding an entrepreneurial venture takes on much broader meaning. First, it is a privilege afforded you by an open, democratic society that cares about your success. Second, it is your chance to take the lead and prove yourself. New venture creation is an unmatched opportunity to earn a sense of accomplishment, self-respect and the respect of others. Third, it is your responsibility to prove that free enterprise works. As you progress, you must pay forward by caring about the success of others, affording them opportunities to prove themselves. You must be compassionate, acting on your concern for the sufferings and misfortunes of others.

James A. Autry says it well in his book, (2001) The Servant Leader: How to Build a Creative Team,

Develop Great Morale and Improve Bottom Line Performance.[2] To Autry, leadership approached properly is a calling. As the leader, "much of the psychological, emotional and financial well-being of other people is dependent on you and on how well you create the circumstances and the environment in which they can do their jobs... If indeed you feel these responsibilities deeply, if the people and their needs engage your own psychological and emotional energies, then you already approach [leadership] as a calling... Leadership in the service of others requires a great deal of courage. It [is]... far easier to be the old top-down kind of boss..."(Autry, pp. xix-xxx)

Autry's bottom line is: "True leadership, unlike management, is not just a set of skills and learned behaviors. What you do as a leader will depend on who you are. And regardless of your own perceptions of yourself, those around you in the workplace – colleagues and employees – can determine who you are only by observing what you do. They can't see inside your head, they can't know what you feel, they can't subliminally detect your compassion or pain or goodwill. In other words, the only way you can manifest your character, your personhood, and your spirit in the workplace is through your behavior." (Autry, p.1)

Consider the broader implications of Autry's good advice. To achieve success, as defined by John Wooden, know that your responsibilities extend beyond leadership of your own ventures. As a leader, you must also work on our free enterprise system to improve it. Part of your pay forward is caring about social improvement and acting on your concerns about social ills.

Riane Eisler explores our responsibilities for social action in her book (2007), The Real Wealth of Nations: Creating a Caring Economics.[3] What is needed, she argues, is a caring economics, one that takes us beyond current economic models "to a way of living, and making a living, that truly meets human needs." (Eisler, p.2)

"As Ghandhi said, we shouldn't mistake what is habitual for what is normal..." "Many of our economic habits were shaped by a warped story of human nature and an economic double standard that gives little or no value to the essential work of caring and caregiving." ..."We have a choice. We can keep complaining about greed, fraud, and cutthroat business practices. We can put up with the daily stress of unsuccessfully juggling jobs and family. We can tell ourselves there's nothing we can do about policies that damage our natural environment, create huge gaps between haves and have nots, and lead to untold suffering. Or we can join together to help construct a saner, sounder, more caring economics and culture." (Eisler, p. 213)

As a principled entrepreneur, how can you succeed by helping others to succeed? We offer you nine links to YouTube clips and websites for your consideration.

First, Narayanan Krishnam is a companion to the forgotten. His caring and compassion is exemplary, as seen in "A Greatly Inspiring Video."[4]

Next, at the venture level, Michael Porter spoke in 2010 on the topic, "Creating Shared Value."[5] Senior corporate executives made up his audience. The occasion was a summit of the Committee Encouraging Corporate Philanthropy (CECP).[6] Porter and the CECP believe private ventures can connect with social challenges to provide a nexus of value, social value, and profits. If you are fortunate enough to work for a CECP member company, check out its donation matching program.

FSG[7] is a nonprofit consulting group that helps public/private partnerships to discover better ways to solve social problems. In 2012, they produced a video entitled, <u>Creating Shared Value, It's the Future</u>.[8] Their website includes client project highlights that show nonprofit, public and private partnerships can have huge impact. Could your venture get involved in a public/private partnership?

Seeking an opportunity where you can personally invest both money and time? Consider Social Venture Partners (SVP).[9] Partners in the SVP Network pool their funds. Together they make multi-year, unrestricted gifts to carefully vetted nonprofit investees with proven potential for social change. Partners also contribute their business and professional expertise to the nonprofits, all with the goal of strengthening the nonprofit and increasing its impact. We offer you a link to a YouTube video clip about SVP, "SVP In Motion."[10]

Do you have more knowledge to share than money, and want to help small business owners? Consider becoming a SCORE mentor.[11] SCORE is a nonprofit association dedicated to helping small businesses get off the ground, grow and achieve their goals through education and mentorship. SCORE members are not just retirees. Some SCORE mentors are college age. Interested? We offer you a link to a short video from the Volunteer page of the SCORE website, "Become a SCORE mentor."[12]

Finally, are you very busy, but want to set aside a

few dollars each month for a good cause? We offer you links to six charities, all respected for their caring, compassion and effective social impact. Click on their logos in the resource folder to learn more.[13]

My grandmother used to say, "A little bit of help is worth a whole lot of pity." Who can you help? Who can your venture help? What can you do today to help make things better at home, at work, or in your community?

Chapter 16: Value Justice and Peace

Supreme Court **CC by 2.0** Chris Phan functoruser

Principle 11 is Value Justice and Peace. Standing for justice and defending the peace means supporting the just rule of law. While good laws and regulations are necessary for advancing free enterprise, they are insufficient to assure justice and good trading. The administration of law must be fair. If citizens widely view it as unfair many things begin to happen. The rule of law breaks down. Win-win deals dwindle. The potential for conflict increases. Overall, attention shifts from adding value to increase economic competitiveness to individual survival. It takes great courage to stand against ill-

advised political winds, blowing one left or right off the legal course to harmonious relations and good trading. However, given human history, support of the just rule of law is practical patriotism.

11. Value Justice and Peace – Justice is the fair administration of law, the act of determining rights and assigning rewards or punishments. Peace is harmonious relations, free from violent disputes. Have the courage to stand for justice and to defend the peace.

Standing for justice and defending the peace are hallmarks of practical patriotism. Why? First, having the courage to stand for justice and to defend the peace is patriotic because it supports an important legacy from our forebears: the just rule of law. The U. S. Constitution recognizes that we have rights. It requires our legal system to protect our rights during legal proceedings.

How important are these rights? We offer you a quick review of the first ten amendments to the Constitution, known as The Bill of Rights. In the resource folder, view a YouTube video entitled, "The Bill of Rights."[1]

[1,2,3,4] See 17-1 to 6 at
http://bit.ly/YourEntrepreneurialJourney

The video was produced by a high school student as a class project.

Our legal justice system is more than the enforcer of political viewpoints. We must assure that both legislation and law enforcement preserve our legacy.

Second, having the courage to stand for justice and defend the peace is pragmatic. It supports the fair administration of law and promotes harmonious relations, free from violent disputes. In short, self-interest requires that we help our legal system to assure that law abiding citizens can peacefully go about their business.

When one thinks about it, the personal and societal consequences of *not* being a practical patriot are scary. Perhaps this is why thoughtful writers from both ends of the political spectrum encourage their readers to be practical patriots. For example, consider the words of Charles G. Koch and John A. Kay.

Charles Koch, in his book (2007), The Science of Success[2], succinctly describes the value of our rule of law. "The rule of law bounds government power and limits its authority to change laws arbitrarily, even when desired by the majority. It also implies that laws must be applied consistently to all, and that all are equal before the law. The rule of law ensures equality of treatment (not equality of outcome), individual freedom and discretion. These lead to civility, prosperity and societal progress. The rule of law, properly applied, secures individual rights, makes the political world more predictable, enables individuals to more easily adapt and leads to behavior that is beneficial to society." (Koch, p.78)

John Kay, in his book (1995) Why Firms Succeed: Choosing Markets and Challenging Competitors to Add Value[3], explores the practical meaning of strategic effectiveness. "It is easy to see why the military analogy continues to exercise such a powerful hold on thinking about corporate strategy.... but it s as misleading as it is helpful.... Business is not like that at all. Success in business derives from add ng value of one's own, not diminishing that of one's competitors', and it is based on distinctive capability, not destructive capability. Distinctive capability becomes harder, not easier, to maintain as size increases. ...[In the military analogy] the equation of scale, power and effectiveness is... often simply assumed, and the generalization from the military to the economic sphere is often assumed to be so obvious as not to require specific elaboration.

"But it is wholly false. Although military strength is directly related to the scale of resources that underpin it, economic strength (whatever that means) is not. If economic strength is competitiveness – and it is hard to see what else it could sensibly mean – then the competitiveness of a nation's industry is related to the aggregate size of its resources of labor, capital, and other factors only in the most tenuous and indirect ways. The smallness of Switzerland, Sweden, and Singapore explains why their military forces will never conquer the world. But it is no obstacle to their firms doing precisely that." (Kay, p.242)

Economic strength is not about conquering. It is about adding value to increase economic competitiveness. It is about envisioning the legal course to harmonious relations and good trading.

Name a country, state, county or city that suffers from widespread corruption. How different might that place be if its citizens and business owners had the courage to support the just rule of law?

Chapter 17: Give Respect

Memorial Day Ceremony - North Africa American Cemetery and Memorial - May 31, 2010 **CC by 2.0** US Army Africa

Principle Twelve is Give Respect. Respect has great importance in everyday life. Many great thinkers have argued about the exact nature of respect and how to give respect. Studying their arguments is important since you must make your own choices about giving respect. We assure you, your choices will be key to your success.

12. Give Respect - John Wooden writes, "Never believe you're better than anybody else, but remember that you're just as good as everybody else." Treat others with dignity, respect, honesty and sensitivity. Encourage and practice teamwork. Appreciate that diversity is valuable. Diversity enables teams to create new ventures that are better than those created by a homogeneous (old boy) network.

Giving respect has great importance in everyday life, including business. We have two reasons for including John Wooden's words in our description of Principle 12. First, as you will read below, this great leader and educator states, in plain words, important truths about giving respect. Second, in our view, during his long years of public service, John Wooden's actions consistently lived up to the full meaning of Principle 12, Give Respect.

The Stanford Encyclopedia of Philosophy includes Robin S. Dillon's extensive survey article, "Respect."[1] (2018 revision) As Dillon points out in the article, great thinkers widely acknowledge that giving respect and self-respect are very important. On the other hand, no settled agreement exists in either everyday thinking, moral or philosophical discussions about respect.

How should we give respect? What are the moral requirements regarding respect? What are the appropriate objects of respect? Similarly, debate is ongoing about the conditions for self-respect. How do we earn self- respect? How do we lose it? (Dillon, page 2 of 54)

Given the importance and the lack of agreement about respect, and how to go about it, you need to evaluate questions of respect for yourself. You need to make your own choices, and we assure you that your choices will be key to your success.

For example, one thing that you might learn is that many self-appointed role models in your life do not measure up. Evaluating questions of respect can

[1,2,3,4,5,6] See 17-1 to 6 at
http://bit.ly/YourEntrepreneurialJourney

literally change your circle of friends and the direction of your life. The Stanford survey article is a great place to start learning more about respect and self-respect. Your choices about respect will be key to your success, informed or not.

What will you learn from further study? For example, consider the words and actions of John Wooden. The roots of Wooden's approach to giving respect go back over 200 years. They may be found in the moral philosophy of Immanuel Kant, (1785) <u>Groundwork of the Metaphysics of Morals in Immanuel Kant Practical Philosophy</u>. The (1996) printing, currently available, is translated and edited by Mary J. Gregor.[2]

Kant was an 18th century German philosopher. He was the first major Western philosopher to put respect for persons, including oneself as a person, at the very center of moral theory.

Kant's writings remain influential to this day. Kant insists that persons are ends in themselves with an absolute dignity whom we must always respect.

We are all too often inclined not to respect persons, not to value them as we should. Kant's formulation of the "Categorical Imperative," which, in his view, is the supreme principle of morality, commands that our actions express due respect for the worth of persons. He argues, "Act in such a way that you treat humanity, whether in your own person or the person of any other, never simply as a means but always at the same time as an end." (Dillon, pp. 2 and 15 of 54) (Kant (1996), p.429)

What are the practical takeaways from the ongoing academic debate about respect? How should we give respect? Who deserves it? How do we earn self- respect? How do we lose it?

Many contemporary bestselling authors offer useful answers for these questions. Consider two examples.

David Brooks shares his views in (2019) The Second Mountain: The Quest for a Moral Life.[3] He speaks of the need for a "sense of common relationships" that leads to voluntary unselfishness, weaving a fabric of reciprocity and trust, and building a better society.

Melinda Gates adds her voice in (2019) The Moment Of Lift: How Empowering Women Changes the World.[4] "The goal is not for everyone to be equal. The goal is for everyone to be connected. The goal is for everyone to belong. The goal is for everyone to be loved.

"Love is what lifts us up. When we come together, we rise. And in the world we're building together, everyone rises. No one is exploited because they are poor or excluded because they're weak. There is no stigma and no shame and no mark of inferiority because you're sick, or because you're old, or because you're not the "right" race, or because you're the "wrong" religion, or because you are a girl or woman. There is no wrong race or religion or gender. We have shed our false boundaries. We can love without limits. We see ourselves in others. We see ourselves *as* others. That is the moment of lift." (page 264)

Personally, we find it helpful to weigh three kinds of respect when choosing how to act. The three are: **Person Respect**, **Earned Respect** and **Self-respect**. The first two refer to our respect for others. The third refers to our respect for ourselves.

Person Respect - Respect each person as a person. This type of respect is not something individuals have to earn or might fail to earn. We owe it to them simply because they are rational beings. We recognize that every stranger has dignity. (Dillon, p. 18 of 54) So does every prospect. For example, you might be a real estate agent holding an open house, an auto salesperson in a car dealership or a volunteer offering remedial education classes at a prison. All prospects who walk in the door are entitled to person respect.

Earned Respect - Give respect to those who earn it. This type of respect is a "status" or "standing" in the community that one earns over time by one's actions. It varies from person to person.

For example, in business organizations, every employee deserves person respect from day one. However, we use earned respect to help organize our reciprocal relations and take care of business.

Ideally, our goal is to base standing or position in the organization on earned respect, rather than on a less utilitarian factor such as cronyism. Effective work groups are formed based on relevant talent, experience and performance and have mutual earned respect. Team leaders are selected, case by case, based on who has the earned respect that will help the team to get its job done.

Self-respect - Respect yourself as a person, decide what you would be, and do what must be done. Person respect and earned respect have to do with the respect of others, and deciding who gets what is often controversial. However, there is surprising agreement among moral and political philosophers about self-respect.

The consensus is that self-respect is something very important in everyday life. We both morally require it and find it essential to the ability to live a satisfying, meaningful, flourishing life - a life worth living. (Dillon, pp. 27-28 of 54)

You may derive self-respect from membership or status in a certain class or social hierarchy. However, earned self-respect seems more important to many – especially successful entre-preneurs. Earned self-respect concerns finding your

Rough, uncut yellow diamond. **CC by Attribution-Share Alike 2.0 Brazil** Eurico Zimbres FGEL/UERJ

worth and merit, based on the quality of your character and conduct. How are you doing? *You* are the judge. (Dillon, p.29 of 54).

To summarize, when it comes to respect, we all start as rough and uncut diamonds. We need work to become the best that we can become – fine gems.

Fancy cut yellow diamond. **CC by 2.0** Fancy Diamonds FancyDiamonds.net

Some parents, teachers, community leaders and bosses consider themselves diamond cutters, cleaving rough stones into fine gems. The reality is that they can lecture to you. They can try to mentor you. They can try to coach you. They can offer you rewards. They can even punish you. However, *you are your own diamond cutter*. You are the master jeweler of your life's work. Success is your choice.

To aid your journey to mastery, we offer you links to a YouTube video and a speech. Produced by Evan Carmichael in 2018, the video is, "9 Ways to Make People Respect You Immediately."[5] It presents nine clips that get to the heart of what respect means.

The speech, "Acres of Diamonds" by Russell H. Conwell is one of the all-time classic pieces of success material.[6] The complete text has been reprinted as an e-book by Project Guttenberg. We highly recommend that you download the speech and read it. According to Conwell, "The idea of the speech is that in this country of ours every man has the opportunity to make more of himself in his own environment, with his own skill, with his own energy, and with his own friends." (Conwell, preface)

Chapter 18: Respect the Earth and Its Creatures

Blue Marble 2000 **CC by 2.0** NASA Goddard Space Flight Center NASA Goddard Photo and Video (Image created by Reto Stockli with the help of Alan Nelson, under the leadership of Fritz Hasler)

Principle Thirteen is Respect the Earth and Its Creatures. It explores what other things besides people we ought to respect. The chapter introduces two ideas that provide useful guidance for action:

"stewardship" and "paradigm shift." It concludes with two examples of the many emerging opportunities for success that derive from adherence to Principle Thirteen.

13. Respect the Earth and Its Creatures – Think globally. Labor to achieve maximum results for all communities at minimum cost to the environment. Embrace sustainability.

In our previous discussion of Principle Twelve, our practical takeaway was that it is helpful to weigh three kinds of respect when choosing how to act in regards to other people. The present question is how should we respect the rest of the world?

The debate continues about "good" answers. In our view, two ideas provide useful guidance for action: "stewardship" and "paradigm shift." For us, the idea of stewardship provides a moral basis for respecting the Earth and its creatures. Assessment of paradigm shifts is one key to deciding what we should respect from a practical point of view.

In his book (2011) The Beginning of Infinity,[1] Oxford physicist David E. Deutsch points out that the Earth

[1, 2, 3, 4, 5, 6, 7, 8] See 18-1 to 8 at
http://bit.ly/YourEntrepreneurialJourney

150

is a small speck in a big, tough universe, and is itself a challenging place to live. Earth's environment is harsh. Survival is a constant struggle for life. Whole species extinction is common. Without hard earned knowledge, humans wouldn't be living in most of the areas where they are now living and would number far less. Most of us depend on life-support systems such as houses, heating, water supply, large scale agriculture, mass production, and goods distribution infrastructure. (Deutsch, pp. 44-45) Our reality includes population pressures, limited resources, and large gaps between haves and have-nots as measured by economic wealth, education, and entrepreneurial opportunities. Given these realities, is Principle Thirteen impractical? We think not for two reasons.

First, despite all, our lives and the world we live in are wondrous gifts given to us unbidden. A short film by Louie Schwartzberg reminds us of our bounty – "Gratitude HD - Moving Art™."[2]

Given the gifts each day brings, two key questions come to mind. Do I choose gratitude for these gifts? Do I wish to preserve these gifts and work to build more to give to my children? Billions of "yes" answers to these two personal questions lead to a global viewpoint that we are all stewards. All of us are morally obliged to preserve and build for future generations. If you wish to be remembered as a great leader, we recommend that you strive to be seen as a good steward first.

The second reason that we think Principle Thirteen is a practical guide to success relates to "foresight" and the "business of paradigms." In our view, present realities offer unprecedented opportunities to entrepreneurs who choose to act constructively, based on foresight and on an understanding of the business of paradigms.

Robert K. Greenleaf in his essay (1970) "The Servant as Leader,"[3] describes foresight as an internal process that deals with intersecting series and random inputs. "Foresight means regarding the events of the instant moment and constantly comparing them with a series of projections made in the past and at the same time projecting future events – with diminishing certainty as projected time runs out into the indefinite future." (Greenleaf, p.13) Greenleaf argues that, as stewards we are morally obliged to develop foresight. "The failure (or refusal) of a leader to foresee may be viewed as an *ethical* failure, because a serious ethical compromise today (when the usual judgement on ethical inadequacy is made) is sometimes the result of a failure to make the effort at an earlier date to foresee today's events and take the right actions when there was a

152

freedom for initiative to act. The action which society labels 'unethical' in the present is often really one of no choice. By this standard a lot of guilty people are walking around with an air of innocence that they would not have if society were able always to pin the label 'unethical' on the failure to foresee and the consequent failure to act constructively when there was freedom to act." (Greenleaf, pp. 13-14)

In his book (1988) <u>Discovering the Future: The Business of Paradigms</u>,[4] Joel Barker approaches the concept of foresight in a different way. He uses the word paradigm and the concept of paradigm shifts to describe how foresight can be translated into business opportunities.

Paradigms are models or patterns that are generally shared by our community. A paradigm is a double-edged sword.

On the one hand it cuts out irrelevancy, explains the world to us, helps us predict its behavior, and guides effective action. On the other hand, when we are in the middle of the paradigm, it is hard to imagine any other paradigm.

When new facts or discoveries do not agree with our current paradigm's established rules and standards, we cut them out as irrelevant. Too often, we are blind to new information that points to needed change and possible solutions.

Today, many of our society's paradigms related to Principle Thirteen appear inadequate to address strong global needs. We need to shift to new paradigms that work better. The shift must happen. It will create unprecedented business opportunities for entrepreneurs who understand what must happen next.

Here is how the paradigm-shift process works. Paradigm creators, often at the fringe of the existing paradigm, invent new paradigms. Entrepreneurial early adopters, seeking solutions, cull through the new paradigms. In a select few, they foresee benefits that outweigh the costs, and discover the future path to profitability. The entrepreneurs shift to the new paradigms. Their new ventures employ the new paradigms to gain comparative advantage, market share and profitability.

Often, industry leaders are reluctant to move away from old paradigms that are "cash cows." However, if they do not adapt to paradigm shifts, they will lose market share and fade away.

Our viewpoint is that the earth's needs are strong. The challenges needing solutions are large. Strong and large enough to offer worthwhile purposes and meaningful rewards to many.

We recommend that you follow Barker's recommendation, "challenge your paradigms on a regular basis by asking the Paradigm Shift question: What do I believe is impossible to do in my field, but, if it could be done, would fundamentally change my business?" (Barker, p. 74)

Paradigm Assessment Practice Set
We offer two (of many) examples of emerging paradigms that may lead to significant paradigm shifts and unprecedented entrepreneurial opportunities. One is global and one is industry specific. Based on these examples, what new enterprise creation opportunities do you foresee?

Example One – The Circular Economy
Over the past few years, (2012-2019), The Ellen MacArthur Foundation commissioned a series of reports about the circular economy.[5] The reports observe an important, global paradigm. Throughout its evolution and diversification, our industrial economy has hardly moved beyond a paradigm established in the early days of industrialization. The paradigm assumes a linear model of resource consumption that follows a "take-make-dispose pattern." The reports advocate that industrial economies shift to a circular paradigm. It argues, "in the quest for a substantial improvement in resource performance across the economy, businesses have started to explore ways to reuse products or their components and restore more of their precious material, energy and labor inputs." (McKinsey and Company, p.6 of the 2012 report)

In June 2012, Stephan Mohr, Ken Somers, Steven Swartz, and Helga Vanthournout published

"Manufacturing Resource Productivity" in the McKinsey Quarterly.[6] The article discusses "how manufacturers can generate new value, minimize cost, and increase operational stability by focusing on four broad areas: production, product design, value recovery, and supply circle management." (Mohr, Somers, Swartz & Vanthournout, p.1) In short, the article describes how to profit by becoming a "circular" company. Of special note is that the coauthors are all part of McKinsey's Sustainability and Resource Productivity Practice. The practice serves major, mainstream enterprises that wish to profit from the circular paradigm.

However, the shifting away from the take-make-dispose paradigm to the circular paradigm did not start in the mainstream. For many years, paradigm creators at the outer fringe of the take-make-dispose paradigm have advocated alternative, circular paradigms. For example, seventeen years ago, William McDonough and Michael Braungart wrote a thought-provoking book on the circular topic. (2002) Cradle to Cradle: Remaking the Way We Make Things.[7]

Today, many entrepreneurial early adopters, have already profited from the circular paradigm. How? They were alert for emerging paradigms at the fringe, foresaw the paradigm shift early, and launched successful enterprises. The emerging paradigm shift toward circular business models is still underway. How might you benefit?

Example Two – IH² Biofuel Technology
In the transportation fuels industry, a new IH² biofuel technology is of interest. It is a catalytic, thermochemical process that promises to be a very cost-effective route to produce liquid transportation fuels. The biofuel paradigm is not new. At the fringes of the transportation fuels industry, many have explored biofuels for several years. However, the new IH² technology has benefits that, in certain cases, may allow it to begin shifting the established fossil-fuel paradigm. It feeds on renewable resources, including solid waste from sewage treatment plants. In small pilot plants, the Gas Technology Institute[8] reported in 2012 that the new technology is self-sufficient. It produces its own hydrogen and a surplus of water. It can operate in a stand-alone configuration anywhere one finds sufficient biomass feed for conversion. Also, the process achieves greenhouse gas reductions of over 90% in comparison to fossil fuels. Projected price at the pump is $2.00 per gallon if efficiencies experienced in pilot plants prove scalable. The target commercial plant output is 300,000 gallons per day.

Do current investments in pilot IH² biofuel plants really foretell a paradigm shift? If so, how might you benefit from it?

Chapter 19: Walk the Talk

"Si, se puede." (Yes, one can) **CC by 3.0 Work Permit**
Source: Cesar_chavez.jpg

Principle Fourteen is Walk the Talk. In this Chapter, we explore the truth contained in an old Persian proverb, "thinking well is wise; planning well, wiser; but doing well is the wisest and best of all."

19. Walk the Talk – Lead by example. Strive to stay true to your values in every action and communication. Use this yardstick: never say or do anything that you would not want your grandchildren to learn about when they come of age.

"Walk the talk" is a popular idiom based on time-tested wisdom. For example, an old Persian proverb reads, "Thinking well is wise; planning well, wiser; but doing well is the wisest and best of all."

In this Chapter we first ask, why is doing well the wisest and best of all? We will draw on the work of three authors to explore this topic. Next, we will ask you five questions about your willingness to walk the talk. We end by offering you three practical resources that will help you build your ventures.

To begin to answer why doing well is the wisest and best of all, consider how the above proverb applies to executives in established firms. Today, as throughout history, too many top level leaders overvalue strategy while undervaluing the importance of innovation and execution. This miscalculation leads to the failure of many C level executives. As an entrepreneur, you can learn from their mistakes.

In his book (2012) <u>Creative Execution: What Great Leaders Do to Unleash Bold Thinking and Innovation</u>[1], Eric Beaudan argues "inevitably, an organization's success hinges not on the strength of its strategy, but on its leaders' ability to craft a realistic view of *how* the strategy will be implemented, and to empower their people to get engaged in its execution in a meaningful way...What CEOs and executives get paid to do is not to lay out a vision and objectives, and then watch their troops perform from the top of the hill." (Beaudan p. 6.)

Of practical interest to entrepreneurs founding new ventures, Beaudan argues that creative execution requires five essential ingredients: (1) A simple, unambiguous strategy, (2) candid dialogue with your team about the strategy and its implementation, (3) clear roles and accountabilities that drive individual and team performance, (4) bold action that puts the strategy into play, and, in our view, perhaps the most important of all (5) your *Visible Leadership* to cement individual

[1,2,3,4,5,6,7,8] See 19-1 to 8 at
http://bit.ly/YourEntrepreneurialJourney

commitments to what your team needs to get done. Without your visible commitment, "the wheels of Creative Execution will spin out of control or take their own separate directions. Visible leadership is required to maintain a common focus, set the pace, keep track of execution successes or failures, and create a positive culture centered on learning and outcomes." (Beaudan, p. 11)

Larry Bossity adds another perspective from the executive suite that has implications for entrepreneurs striving to learn how to do well. In 2002, he published (2002) Execution: The Discipline of Getting Things Done.[2] At the time, Bossity was Chairman and former CEO of Honeywell International, with a career-long string of C level positions to his credit. In his view, "Every great leader has had an instinct for execution. He has said, in effect, 'unless I can make this plan happen, it's not going to matter." Too many high level thinkers,"are articulate conceptualizers, very good at grasping strategies and explaining them. This, they know is what it takes to get ahead. They aren't interested in the 'how' of getting things done: that's for somebody else to think about." (Bossity, p. 35). "...The intelligent, articulate conceptualizers don't necessarily understand how to execute. Many don't realize what needs to be done to convert a vision into specific tasks, because their high level thinking is too broad. They don't follow through and get things done; the details bore them. They don't crystallize thought or anticipate roadblocks. They don't know how to pick people for their organizations who can execute. Their lack of engagement deprives them of the sound judgment about people that comes only through practice." (Bossity, p.36)

In his book (2010) <u>Staying Power: Six Enduring Principles for Managing Strategy and Innovation in an Uncertain World</u>[3], Michael A. Cusumano's third principle is "Capabilities, Not Just Strategy." "Managers should focus not simply on formulating strategy or a vision of the future (that is deciding what to do) but equally on building distinctive organizational capabilities and operational skills (that is, how to do things) that rise above common practice (that is, what most firms do). Distinctive capabilities center on people, processes, and accumulated knowledge that reflect a deep understanding of the business and the technology, and how they are changing. Deep capabilities, combined with strategy, enable the firm to offer superior products and services as well as exploit foreseen and unforeseen opportunities for innovation and business development." (Cusumano, p. 114)

Take time now to distill the good advice contained in the above comments. Ask yourself, are you willing to walk the talk?

Before you answer, consider five questions:
1. *Is success your choice?*
2. *If you want it, can you make it happen?*
3. *Are you willing to do more than just think about success and plan it?*
4. *Are you willing to learn what you need to know to get things done?*
5. *Are you willing to do what you have to do to succeed?*

If you are willing to walk the talk, we offer you four practical resources to help you succeed.

First, Loretta Malandro gives you her nine communication rules for unleashing your personal power and achieving success in her book, (2015) <u>Speak Up, Show Up, and Stand Out: The 9 Communication Rules You Need to Succeed.</u>[4] She concludes the book with wise words that get to the heart of what Principle 14 "Walk the Talk" entails.

"You have to see yourself as the person you want to be before you can become that person. You must have an ideal you aspire to in order to push yourself.

Your vision of you must be compelling, strong and decisive." (Malandro, p. 247)

In order to create this vision for yourself you must: "Own your experiences, actions, words, and reactions. You are in charge of you…. You live by the code of 100% accountability.

"Have the courage to stand up for who you are and take accountability, not blame for how your words and actions affect others.

"Accept that you have imperfections; you're human just like the rest of us. And you embrace the fact that being effective is far more important to you than your need to be right.

"Excel at being bigger than any circumstance. Even in the most difficult situations, you remember who you are and what you stand for. You break down barriers by being authentic, talking straight responsibly, and recovering quickly and rebounding stronger than ever." (Malandro, p.247)

Captain D. Michael Abrashoff (USN ret.) published the second resource in 2002. It is a national bestseller that remains a favorite of many leadership coaches. Abrashoof walks the talk. The revised edition of his book, (2012) It's Your Ship:

168

<u>Management Techniques from the Best Damn Ship in the Navy</u>[5], *is a practical, how to, guide on doing what Eric Beaudan calls visible leadership.*

The third resource is, (1975) "The Goya Effect."[6] It is a classic, short film on how to manage by walking around. The film is hard to find. In case you get lucky, we will not give away the plot. Here, we will share the advice street-wise managers give to the male protagonist in the film. He is not unlike many entrepreneurs we know.

Do not, "overemphasize systems and figures. They are valuable for forward planning, but do not reveal what is happening now." Frequently walk around the workplace. Look for "things happening that should not be, and also for things that are not noticed simply because they are always there....It is a question of noticing what is happening at the sharp end and then finding out why." (Meeting Guide: The Goya Effect, p.8)

As you do this, it is important to read the "signals that people give both consciously and unconsciously." It is also important to remember "that the question of signals works both ways, and [you]... must learn to give the right signals to [your]... people." (Meeting Guide: The Goya Effect, p. 9)

As you walk around the workplace, do six things to give the right signals:

*"**First** – have a reason for being there. The more you're there the more reasons you will have. But to start with, find a reason or you will be self-conscious and behave like a visiting V. I. P.*

*"**Second** – what you do is as important as what you say. For instance– stand alongside people, don't confront them across their work, and be interested, really interested. The more interested you are, the more you will engage other people's interest, and the more they'll respond.*

*"**Third** – look and listen; really look and listen consciously. It's hard work – at first you have to keep reminding yourself to make the effort, but after awhile it becomes second nature.*

*"**Fourth** – Don't cross examine people. Ask for help, get them to explain things, then they talk their own way, more freely: and when you make notes it should be what they want you to remember – make your own notes afterwards.*

*"**Fifth** – Talk about work. That is all you will have in common to start with. You won't win their trust by asking about Grannie's lumbago, you will win it by caring about them in their jobs, and in time that will earn you the right to their personal confidences.*

*"**Sixth** – and above all – follow through. If someone has an idea you can act on do so and tell them how it's going. If you can't act on it, tell them why not."*

(Meeting Guide: The Goya Effect, pp. 9-10).

We conclude this chapter with a fourth resource. It is a link to a YouTube video. The video is about an entrepreneurial child named Caine Monroy and his dad George. It is a practical demonstration of what can happen if you walk the talk. The video is entitled, "Caine's Arcade." [7]

(p.s. The last time we checked, this video went viral with over seven million YouTube views. A follow-up video has over one million views. Caine, now a teenager raised over $250,000 for his college fund. Also, the first customer of Caine's arcade Nirvan Mullick (who also produced the videos) started the Imagination Foundation which has reached over one million children in eighty countries with its "Global Cardboard Challenge" and other initiatives. Much more has happened. Read all about it at cainesarcade.com.[8])

Chapter 20: Strive for Success

Nelson Mandela Courtesy of "South Africa The Good News" www.sagoodnews.co.za

Principle Fifteen is Strive for Success. In this chapter we discuss what it means to strive, how striving relates to courage and persistence, and to our strengths and weaknesses.

20. Strive for Success - Produce results that create value to realize your full potential and find fulfillment in your work. Success is within you. It's up to you to bring it out. Success comes from making the effort to become the best of which you are capable. Strive to improve a little each day, eventually big things will occur. Lasting success is not the big, quick, improvement. Rather, it results from small improvements one day at a time. Success is not perfection. One can never reach perfection. Nevertheless, perfection is the goal.

Strive is the key word in Principle Fifteen. It has five definitions: "to struggle in opposition," "to contend," "to fight vigorously," "to make great efforts," "to devote serious effort or energy."

Most people feel they are principled. Many consciously adopt guiding principles. Yet, few fulfill their success potential. Why?

In our view, the answer is that most of us do not *strive* consistently. We imagine success. We dream about how pleasant it will be when we are successful.

We read about success and feel inspired by Carol Dweck's discussion of growth mindsets or John Wooden's description of how to achieve competitive greatness.

We may even plan pathways to success in our personal and professional lives. Sometimes, we act to carry out our plans.

However, even when we act, we often move forward timidly, retreating at the first mishap, rather than learning from the experience and trying again. Most of us do not *strive* consistently.

For example, consider your exercise program. We offer you a link to a YouTube clip entitled, "Running."[1]

The "Running" YouTube clip would ring true for Psychologist Angela Duckworth. She argues that for anyone striving to succeed—be it athletes or business people—the secret to outstanding achievement is not talent but a special blend of passion and persistence she calls "grit." (2016) Grit: The Power of Passion and Perseverance [2]

Striving implies courage and persistence. Resolute effort to improve by long hours of determined practice and learning from many "failures." One cannot permit fear of failure to prevent effort.

Many years ago, David Eisenman told a story from early in his career about one of his students (who we will call Chris). David is the founder of the Mardan School in Irvine, California.[3] Mardan is a

[1,2,3,4,5,6,7] See 20-1 to 7 at
http://bit.ly/YourEntrepreneurialJourney

therapeutic school. It combines a rigorous academic curriculum with therapeutic supports, social skills instruction, and necessary interventions as part of the regular school day.

Chris' parents took Chris to a tennis match. The next day, Chris approached David overflowing with excitement about the experience. "I want to be a tennis champion," Chris exclaimed.

David, sadly and carefully explained to Chris that learning to play tennis would be extremely difficult. David recommended that Chris try alternative sports where he could employ his strengths. Armed with David's coaching, Chris headed toward the school gym with a determined look in his eye.

(Why was David hesitant? Due to a physiological condition, Chris' medical doctors reported that Chris had very limited hand-eye coordination. Chris could not do many things most of us take for granted, like hitting a ball with a racket. The normal nerve connections simply were not there.)

Months later, Chris knocked on the door of David's office. On entering, beaming with pride, Chris held up a sports trophy. "I won!" Chris said. David asked cheerfully "Congratulations. What Sport?" "Tennis" Chris replied.

David will never forget the lesson he learned from Chris. Never assume failure. *Striving* can lead to success. Courage and persistence often allow us to strengthen alternative connections within us that allow us to magnify and redeploy our strengths. Through striving we learn to overcome or work around obstacles, ranging from internal weaknesses to external threats.

Nineteen hundred years ago, Epictetus said, "First say to yourself what you would be; and then do what you have to do." Often striving is extremely difficult. For example, as entrepreneurs, whether we want to or not, we must lead to succeed.

Like Chris, the tennis player, successful entrepreneurs are not perfect. However, they must strive to become exceptional leaders. They do so, not by focusing 100% on correcting their leadership weaknesses, but by developing their unique and profound strengths.

Chris, the tennis player, had a choice. Chris could try to correct a big weakness. For example, the physiological inability to hit the ball like "normal" people. Or, Chris could strive to develop strengths to win matches. Chris chose winning. By striving, he found how to work around a "fatal" weakness.

In this, we all know Chris is not alone. We offer you a link to two YouTube videos. Like Chris' story, they are reminders to not let yourself define your "differences" as bad – imagine yourself beyond what others see. Your differences are what make you special. We recommend you bookmark these two videos in your browser. The first one is: "Life = Risk."[4] The Second is, "What Makes You Special."[5]

As entrepreneurs, striving develops our leadership strengths. We each strive in our own way, but the result of our striving often has marked, positive impact on bottom-line results and employee performance.

In their book (2012) How to Be Exceptional: Drive Leadership Success by Magnifying Your Strengths,[6] John Zenger, Joseph Folkman, Robert Sherwin and Barbara Steel emphasize strengths. They base their emphasis on their research.

In their words, "Our decision to emphasize the development of strengths is based on [three] factors. First, the...data show that regardless of how much effort people spend on correcting weaknesses, it will only bring them to a certain midpoint on the overall measure of effectiveness.

"Second,...our preoccupation with fixing weaknesses causes managers to focus on asking people to improve capabilities based solely on the fact that they are weaknesses, rather than their importance to the success of an individual.

"[Third,] Oftentimes capabilities that will make a person eminently successful are things we already do fairly well, but when these capabilities are improved, they would lead to dramatically more success." (Zenger, et al., p.39)

According to Zenger, Folkman, Sherwin, and Steel Zenger, there are four benefits from building on strengths:

"1. People are more motivated when they work on their strengths. It will come as no surprise that when people work on something they enjoy, they are more willing to invest time and effort into improvement.

"2. Those who worked on their strengths were more successful in their change efforts, and that substantially increased their overall leadership effectiveness.

"3. Change in outcomes – such as employee commitment, intention to stay, highly committed

employees, total sales, and performance ratings –
followed improvements in leadership effectiveness.

"4. Such improvement provides incentive and
motivation for further development." (Zenger, et al.,
p.89)

When it comes down to it, standard text paragraphs
cannot bring home the full meaning of what it
means to strive for success. To conclude this final
chapter about Mihaylo Entrepreneurship's Fifteen
Guiding Principles, we offer you a short poem and
one final YouTube clip.

Rapids **CC by -SA 2.0** Anne Hornyak anneh662

Ready for Success?

Courage and persistence
find pathways
around weakness.
To strength.
To success.

Decide what you would be.
Obstacles?
The root breaks the rock.
Wind and water triumph over stone.

Strive.
Set to it like flowing water,
torrent, quiet stream, or drip.
As needs be.
Always steady.
Unstoppable.

The final YouTube clip is "Coldplay Performs
"Imagine" ft. (Emmanuel Kelly)"[7]

Think about a competition that you want to win (or a venture you want to launch). Are you worried that you might not qualify for entry? Try anyway! You cannot finish until you start. Give yourself permission to succeed. Step forward, strive, and earn success.